ALSO BY TIM WU

The Master Switch
The Attention Merchants
The Curse of Bigness

THE AGE OF EXTRACTION

THE AGE OF EXTRACTION

HOW TECH PLATFORMS
CONQUERED THE ECONOMY AND
THREATEN OUR FUTURE PROSPERITY

TIM WU

ALFRED A. KNOPF   NEW YORK   2025

A BORZOI BOOK
FIRST HARDCOVER EDITION
PUBLISHED BY ALFRED A. KNOPF 2025

Published by Alfred A. Knopf,
a division of Penguin Random House LLC,
1745 Broadway, New York, NY 10019.

Knopf, Borzoi Books, and the colophon are registered trademarks
of Penguin Random House LLC.

Library of Congress Cataloging-in-Publication Data
Names: Wu, Tim, author.
Title: The age of extraction : how tech platforms conquered the economy and
threaten our future prosperity / Tim Wu.
Description: First edition. | New York : Alfred A. Knopf, 2025. |
Includes bibliographical references and index.
Identifiers: LCCN 2024060501 | ISBN 9780593321249 (hardcover) |
ISBN 9780593321256 (ebook) | ISBN 9781524712952 (open-market)
Subjects: LCSH: Multi-sided platform businesses. | Artificial
intelligence—Economic aspects. | Technological innovations—Moral and
ethical aspects. | Technological unemployment.
Classification: LCC HD9999.M782 .W82 2025 |
DDC 338.7—dc23/eng/20250327
LC record available at https://lccn.loc.gov/2024060501

penguinrandomhouse.com | aaknopf.com

Printed in the United States of America
1st Printing

The authorized representative in the EU for product safety and compliance
is Penguin Random House Ireland, Morrison Chambers, 32 Nassau Street,
Dublin D02 YH68, Ireland, https://eu-contact.penguin.ie.

For Essie

CONTENTS

THE AGE OF EXTRACTION

INTRODUCTION

In the spring of 2024, Apple briefly ran an extraordinary advertisement. It depicted various instruments of cultural achievement—books, a record player, an upright piano—all being crushed by a giant press. A trumpet, on its end, was twisted and bent; a piano collapsed, and paint cans exploded. By the end, everything had been magically reduced into a single device—an iPad—which was described as "the thinnest Apple product yet."[1]

"The only thing that could have made it more dystopian," wrote one commentator, "would have been if actual human beings had been playing the instruments, reading the books, or wielding the paintbrushes."[2] Apple quickly announced that the advertisement was not intended to send any larger message. But as Freud once said about jokes, advertisements often reveal uncomfortable truths. And the truth referred to in that advertisement is one we all know: that we live in a time where human experience has been transformed. The spectacle of human achievement crushed into a tiny device, possessed of its own intelligence, resonates with something we are all experiencing—a sense that as we augment humanity, we may, at the same time, have come to marginalize actual humans.

It was at roughly the same time that the artificial intelligence firm OpenAI debuted a new voice that sounded strikingly similar to actress Scarlett Johansson.[3] Johansson had previously refused offers to license her voice, but apparently the firm went ahead and created a replica anyway. She is in a better situation than the golfer Jack Nicklaus, however, who sold the rights to his name and likeness and has been unable to control the conduct of an AI-replica named "Digital Jack," operated by a firm named Soul Machines.[4] It speaks to the apparent replaceability of even the most famous of humans.

The fears of our diminished importance arrive at a time when many Americans have come to feel a parallel sense of economic marginalization. Over the last quarter century, even when the economy has been healthy by traditional indicators, a great majority of Americans remain doubtful about their economic future. Many younger Americans went to college, worked hard, and still cannot afford decent housing. They fear being worse off than their parents, something once unheard of in this land. The contrast with corporate citizens is stark; many American corporations seem to have escaped any usual orbit and blasted off into an outer space of perpetual profit, bringing their executives along for the ride.

We must see that the problems of technological and economic marginalization are entwined. Technology has never been neutral, but rather reflects ideology and what it is designed to do. Today's great tech platforms are impressive, entertaining, and convenient, but also designed to be some of history's most advanced tools for extracting wealth and resources from the broader economy. Consequently, as they become essential to everything, we are at risk of building an economy that is perpetually unfair for much of humanity.

The phrase "wealth extraction" is the key to this book. It refers to the ability to take money from everyone else and is born of being essential and unavoidable. As the tech platforms have grown and evolved over the last decade, they have focused their attention on refining their methods of extraction. In return for an undeniable and unescapable utility, they are fine-tuned to take as much as possible—data, attention, profit margins—from everyone else.

We remain in the early days of platform capitalism and commercially relevant artificial intelligence. But we risk falling into a two-class age, where many industries become divided into two groups: the extractors and their agents on the one side; dependent businesses, consumers, and employees on the other. There is every reason to fear living in a future with a technologically armored wall between the haves and have-nots. We should also fear a future in which the private power and wealth aggregated in the tech platforms comes to influence and combine with the public powers of government.

The main goal of this book, then, is to help readers understand the emergent form of economic power in our time—the artificially intelligent tech platform. You may already work in an industry deeply influenced by platforms or have had your life affected by them in other ways. If not, you should know: they are probably coming for you.

This book also aims to answer a question: Just what happened to the broad spread of prosperity and democracy many expected to follow the Internet revolution? Back in the 1990s and 2000s, many believed that the popular Internet would make everyone better off in an evenhanded manner while spreading democracy around the world. That was wrong: a handful of platforms and owners have taken the lion's share of the new cash, and it is autocracy, not democracy, that is on the rise. If we are to imagine a better future, we need to understand what happened and why those prophecies did not come to pass.

To that end—in order to understand our past and our future—this book begins by explaining the origins of platform power. The power of the tech platforms relies on ancient economics: there have been essential platforms in every civilization. Platform power also bears some similarity to other historic forms of economic power, such as land ownership and the industrial power of manufacturing. But platform power is distinct from both of these, as its power does not lie in production but rather in catalysis. It resides in the *hosting* of economic activity and the *extraction* of value, including the *harvesting* of specialized assets like data and human attention. As we shall explain, the tech platforms have combined old principles and new technologies to become the ascendant economic powers of our time. That's why few can ignore what it will mean for the ongoing transformation of the United States and the world.

IS THIS A PROBLEM THAT SOLVES ITSELF?

Some may find the preceding paragraphs much too gloomy and pessimistic. Technological advance and prosperity have always gone hand in hand, after all. Surely we should expect advances in platform technology and artificial intelligence to make humanity wealthier and happier. Even if some have ended up with a little more right now, we ought to expect everyone to benefit over the long run. This particular brand of tech optimism has well-known adherents. Jeff Bezos, Amazon's founder, has repeatedly suggested that we live in the best of times. Marc Andreessen, a venture capitalist well known in Silicon Valley, writes that "there is no material problem—whether created by nature or by technology—that cannot be solved with more technology."[5]

Sam Altman, the CEO of OpenAI, is among those who believe that technological advances are our best solution to the problems of uneven wealth. To his credit, he takes seriously the fact that humanity is suffering from a spread of inequality. He is the cofounder of a group known as "Tools for Humanity," which identifies humanity's "grand challenges" as "global income inequality, governance of existential risks, and distinguishing humans from artificial intelligence."[6]

Altman argues that improving artificial intelligence is the clearest way to solve economic inequalities and the problem of poverty. In a manifesto written in September 2024, Andreessen wrote that once we achieve better AI, "we can have shared prosperity to a degree that seems unimaginable today."[7] In an interview with author Nate Silver, Altman said, "If you have something like an AGI [artificial general intelligence], I think poverty really does just end."[8]

I take Altman as well-meaning and there is an admirable optimism in this declaration. But it is, at best, a statement of faith. History, unfortunately, gives us a more realistic picture of the impact of new technologies on the distribution of wealth in society. It is unquestionably true that technological change creates wealth. It is the division of those spoils that has always been the tricky part. And too often, technological advances have been used to widen, not narrow, economic divides.

There have certainly been technologies, such as the agricultural plow, that have spread new productivity and wealth to property owners around the world. But there have been other technologies, such as the cotton gin, that have taken a bad situation and made it worse. In the case of the cotton gin—which perpetuated plantation slavery—the problem wasn't the technology itself but the economic structure of the American South.

The nations that have actually succeeded in sustaining long-term growth and equality have not, historically, taken a trickle-down approach. For example, the United States has taken very different approaches at different times. During its best and most forward-thinking years, the United States actually sought to balance economic power, whether through the broad distribution of land and other productive assets, the breaking up of monopolies, protecting worker organizing, or building a social safety net. But during our worst years, we have just accepted a centralization of economic power, as in slave states before the Civil War, or the tolerance of monopolies in the 1890s and 1920s. The latter approach has not gone well, in the United States or elsewhere.

It is unscientific to take technology as some kind of omnibenevolent godhead that will act by itself to solve humanity's problems. What technology will do for us depends on how we design it and where economic power resides. That's why the real challenge for humanity is to design an economic future that works for more people, rather than assuming that future will just arrive someday.

THE BETTER ALTERNATIVE: STRUCTURAL BALANCING

The U.S. Constitution was predicated on a deep suspicion of all forms of unaccountable power. The revolutionaries had witnessed firsthand the brutality of both British monopoly and colonial government. The Constitution's approach, engineered by James Madison, depends on structural balancing. It did not assume that power would dissipate naturally. Instead, it divides and balances power to avoid the dangers of tyranny. It aims to respect freedoms while constantly seeking balance. Even though the Constitution was mainly concerned with public power, that same Madisonian tradition holds the key to our economic future. Power is power, whether private or public.

You may be skeptical that the concept of balance has any place in American commerce, given that capitalism is said to thrive on animal passions. You might think that balance would hinder growth or dampen incentives. But when done well, this is simply not true. Take as an example an institution that could not be more American or commercial, yet puts economic balancing at its core. That institution is the National Football League.

It may be surprising to hear it, but the United States' National Football League has long embraced the kind of balancing favored by figures like James Madison. It is a simple fact that a city like Los Angeles or New York has a larger local media audience than a city like Kansas City or Baltimore. Without balancing, the teams in large, rich cities would employ all the best players and dominate their rivals. It would be a two-class league: divided between perpetual winners and losers.

The NFL intervenes strongly to prevent that outcome. It wisely avoids interventions that might seem unfair, like giving smaller cities a ten-point lead. The interventions are, instead, structural, centered on salary caps, the draft, and schedule. The league also has a strong union that bargains collectively for the players, and the league divides advertising revenue evenly among teams. The result is that a city that is smaller and less wealthy, like Kansas City, can compete with giant metropolises—and win.

Some might consider the NFL's rules to be heavy-handed. But does the NFL embrace fairness at the price of prosperity? The answer is no: the NFL is the most valuable sports league in the world. More generally, as *The Wall Street Journal* points out, American sports leagues are more valuable than the unbalanced European leagues, despite having smaller audiences.[9] The point is that prosperity, fairness, and growth are not incompatible. And when it comes to nations, as the World Bank affirms, it is the more equitable, economically balanced countries that tend to be wealthier on a per capita basis.

Structural balancing, done correctly, speaks to an enlightened self-interest that can yield greater wealth and prosperity for all. As Tocqueville wrote in the 1830s, Americans "are fond of explaining almost all the actions of their lives by the principle of interest rightly understood."[10] They explain "how an enlightened regard for themselves constantly prompts them to assist each other." We would be an even wealthier country if we could draw on the full potential of the entire population, and not just a few regions, classes, or companies.

THE PROMISE OF A PLATFORM ECONOMY

Our extraordinary technological revolutions have given humanity great abundance. For the first time in history, we have the ability to create a sustainable and happy prosperity for all. Jeff Bezos was correct that we have more than ever before, with technologies capable of producing more than enough for everyone.

What we don't have is the structure—an architecture of equality to match current technological realities. The program outlined in this book calls for strong anti-monopoly policies meant to curb obvious and illegal aggregation of power. This is a project that I've been personally involved in for more than a decade, and one that is underway in the 2020s with American and European lawsuits against Google, Amazon, Facebook, and others. But for the longer term, we need neutrality rules for platforms that both preserve the economic flourishing that platforms catalyze and also stop those same platforms from extracting too much from everyone else.

What this book will show you is how we can do it. That means a journey with several steps. First, it is essential to learn the basics of platform economics. The neutral platform is the foundation of any broadly prosperous society, being a structure that catalyzes economic activity. But it can also become an instrument of undue wealth extraction, as we learned in the age of the railroads, and as we are learning again today. The next step is to understand the specific history of today's tech platforms: the first computing and communications platforms run by IBM and AT&T, and the government interventions that forced them to serve the broader economy. From that point, we can understand the current generation of platforms—Google, Facebook, Amazon, Microsoft, and the rest—and their adoption of the business models we experience today. The second half of the book takes a step back to understand the dangers of centralized economic power over a broader historic context, examining what kind of interventions have worked and will work to restructure the economy.

A large and wealthy middle class is key to our future prosperity. It has been, at times, America's trademark, and it should be our goal. If we do it right, tech platforms will actually play a major role in creating and sustaining a broadly wealthy country, and also in creating an economic model worth exporting to the rest of the world. But if we get things wrong, we risk a future in which our technologies actively worsen the division and resentment that are the curse of our age.

PART I

UNDERSTANDING PLATFORM POWER

Not so long ago, in the early 2000s, we lived in an age of extraordinary optimism about the Internet and what it would do for all of us. It would interconnect all humanity, give everyone a creative outlet, and make democracy blossom around the world. Economically and socially, it would empower the little guys—favor entrepreneurial individuals—at the expense of faceless corporations. As tech pundit Jeff Jarvis wrote in 2009, "small is the new big."[1] He wrote that "a tiny start-up can become a manufacturing company using somebody else's factory and distribution while selling to a worldwide market. [. . .] Any of us can start a highly specialized and targeted media company using blog software. [. . .] The Lilliputians have triumphed. The economies of scale must now compete with the economies of small."[2]

Jarvis was hardly alone in his optimism. Business writer Seth Godin titled an entire book *Small Is the New Big* (2006). Professor Yochai Benkler, then at Yale, argued that self-organizing production systems would compete with and possibly overcome managerial or price-driven systems.[3] Richard Florida's 2003 *The Rise of the Creative Class* assumed a world in which creators would easily become the agents of their own economic destiny. One way or another, the message was the same: in the Internet age, the spoils would belong to everyone.

Not very often are so confident a set of predictions so wrong. The reason they were wrong is important to this book and essential to learn from. The key mistake was a failure to truly understand platforms and their unique brand of power. For these writings and projections came at a time when several open platforms—the Web, the Internet, a disciplined Microsoft—really did favor the little guy. But it was not to last, as we shall see.

What these writers did not predict is that it would not be the little guys who prospered, but their hosts—a new generation of platforms that would find ingenious ways to take the lion's share of the Internet economy for themselves. To understand this point and how it happened, we must back up to introduce the very basics of platform economics.

CHAPTER 1

THE GENIUS OF THE ANCIENT CITY SQUARE

Everything needs to happen somewhere. That is why every civilization has had specialized spaces that facilitate commerce, speech, and other activities. In ancient Greece, the town square, or "agora," served not just for buying and selling stuff but also for religious festivals, entertainment, and government.[1] The bazaar was invented in the Middle East and much of commerce in ancient China centered on the market-town, or 市. These are the ancestors of today's tech platforms, and we need to understand what gave them their economic significance.

It might help to better define what we mean by a "platform." (The English word comes from the French *platte fourme* or "flat form.") It can be described as any space or structure that in one way or another brings together two or more groups to transact or interact while reducing the costs of doing so. They can be buyers and sellers, but also readers and publishers, listeners and speakers. And as the French word suggests, a platform usually implied a certain evenhandedness.

This definition of a platform covers a lot of ground. It covers the most ancient form of transactional platform just described: the city marketplace. The term encompasses more, including stock exchanges, suburban shopping malls, and the Tokyo fish market, all of which bring together buyers and sellers. And as we shall see later, it also includes so-called enabling platforms that allow their buyers and sellers to do things they otherwise could not.

A CATALYTIC SPACE

In chemistry, a catalyst is anything that initiates or accelerates a chemical reaction without being affected itself. The operation of many complex natural systems—like most of the biochemistry that keeps us alive—is largely a story of catalysis.

The same is true in the economy: it is the catalysts that matter most. Selling does not simply "happen" if the price is right. The conditions must be right. It is this power—a catalytic power—that platforms harness.

Stated more formally, the most basic function of the platform is to enable mutually beneficial transactions—and thereby generate wealth or the satisfaction of human wants and needs. Platforms do so by solving not just one but several barriers that otherwise prevent transactions from occurring.* Consider four major challenges that a successful platform addresses.

First Problem: Matching

I used to have a fig tree in my backyard, and when the time came, it bore a lot of fruit. A good fig tree will actually produce far more output than any one family can eat. In economic terms, a fig tree creates a surplus. In fact, most agricultural holdings create a surplus relative to family consumption.

The existence of a surplus creates the potential for trade—

---

* Lowering transaction costs, in other words. Readers with a background in economics will recognize that this is a point similar to that made in Oliver Williamson's *Transaction Cost Economics*. However, Williamson largely focused on the advantages that an integrated firm might have, as opposed to the reduction of transaction costs between unrelated parties.

here, selling excess produce to buyers. In a basic economics class, it is common to assume that the matching of buyers and sellers happens automatically, if the buyer values it more than the seller. If so, the transaction happens, as if by magic.

In real life, as it isn't always easy to match buyers and sellers, extra produce is often just left to rot. It is the facilitation of such transactions—the existence of marketplaces—that makes all the difference. The successful matching of buyers and sellers is required to make transactions happen. That is why platforms and marketplaces are so key to successful economies.

In this matchmaking function lies much of the value in a platform. In the language of platform economics popularized by French economist Jean Tirole, the platform exists to bring two "sides" of a market together.[2] The more buyers and sellers a platform can muster, the more valuable it is. More buyers and more sellers attract more of each, in a version of what is sometimes called "network effects."[*] As economist David Evans writes in *Matchmakers*, platform businesses have as "raw materials [. . .] the different groups of customers that they help bring together."

Think how often advertising for a business conference relies on *who* will be there. Social media start-ups that fail to reach a critical mass don't make it; this is one of the reasons that a site like Facebook, despite the many scandals, whistleblowers, and privacy violations, keeps chugging along, as it still has everyone on it.

Sometimes a platform may have trouble attracting enough members of one side of a transactional pair. Often it is buyers who are scarce: when I worked in industry, I recall going to trade shows that were all sellers of equipment and no buyers and were therefore considered a bust. In the old days, a party with too many men and too few women was called a "sausage fest." Sophisticated platform operators often try to subsidize the missing side, or even pay one group to show up. Hence the practice of paying

---

[*] "Network effects" (or externalities) refers to the idea that a network may become more valuable the more people use it and was originally used to describe services like telephone networks. In the platform context such effects are important, and are also found on both sides of the platform: i.e., more buyers attracts more sellers, which attracts more buyers and so on.

celebrities to appear at parties, or the old practice—banned in some cities—of offering a gender-based discount ("ladies' night") to attract more women to a bar.

Jumping ahead a little, it is clear that in our times matching remains a core function of tech platforms. Every tech platform is at some level in the business of connecting people and businesses. It can be worth losing money on one side or—even for a time—both sides of the transaction. For years, Uber gave everyone rides that were effectively below cost so as to build up the network. And now you can understand one reason that there's so much "free" stuff on platforms like Google and Facebook: it is the free drink that draws in users so they might meet . . . advertisers.

Second Problem: Information and Trust

Ever consider buying a Persian rug only to be put off by the difficulty of ascertaining what, exactly, you might be getting? Or want to purchase something but have no idea how to get started? Information gaps also prevent transactions from happening in more than one way. To buy something, you need to know, at a minimum, that the product exists and what its price is. For more significant purchases, a buyer also needs to know that the product is of acceptable quality. In a farmers market, the appearance of the product—red tomatoes or green lettuce—conveys a lot. But observing quality can be a subtle thing. Does that used car have an engine that is about to quit? Is that Persian carpet actually from Persia? Is that company selling stock about to go bankrupt?

The seller almost always knows more than the buyer, creating an imbalance (technically, an asymmetry). The owner of an apartment with a train line nearby knows that passing trains will rattle the windows and wake you up, even if you don't know that. That prospect of unknown (and bad) information can itself deter sales for fearful buyers. I suspect many people don't buy Persian rugs or used cars precisely because they fear being cheated in one way or another. As economist George Akerlof theorized in a famous 1970 paper, that fear of being cheated or even defrauded can itself function to deter transactions, even if the product is actually fine.[3]

Since antiquity, platforms have helped solve such informational problems, either by themselves or with the help of the law. In the ancient Athenian agora, the city maintained standard weighing scales and expelled fraudulent sellers. In today's stock markets, those who wish to sell securities are required to disclose copious amounts of information intended to ensure that buyers understand the risks of buying stocks. Today's online marketplaces usually use review systems to try to give buyers a sense of underlying quality.

None of these fixes are perfect. Investors still get cheated, and who hasn't bought a product that turned out to be a dud, despite glowing reviews? The goal, however, is to mitigate the problem sufficiently so that buyers buy with confidence, and transactions happen—and platforms do a lot to help.

Third Problem: Making Small Business Big—Reducing Minimal Scale

On East 11th Street in the East Village of New York, there is a tiny store named Casey's that sells nothing but rubber stamps in several hundred patterns. On the Amazon Marketplace, there is a three-man Canadian firm named Bananaphone that only sells a banana-shaped telephone handset.

Successful platforms also make it easier for smaller and highly specialized operations to do business. Put differently, and more technically, a platform can reduce the minimal necessary scale of operation, by reducing what a smaller operation needs to sell its products or services.

Take our owner of the abundant fig tree. Given a local farmers market, all she really needs is a stall. She does not need an advertising budget, a store, or distribution services. Taken a few steps further, a relatively small farmer—like one of my cousins, who operates an entire wheat and soybean farm herself—can use different platforms to sell her produce, and even, using supply chains, ship soybeans to buyers on different continents.

On the "enabling platforms"—usually forms of infrastructure—
this effect is most pronounced. Enabling platforms are those that
make sellers (and sometimes users) capable of doing things that
they cannot do otherwise. A classic example is a transportation
platform, like the canal and rail networks of the nineteenth century, which made possible selling at greater distances. Most tech
platforms are enabling platforms. The game console, for example, gives software developers the tools to create an entertainment product. Ride-sharing platforms give drivers an awareness
of which individuals are looking for rides, and vice versa.

This "reducing-minimum-scale" role played by open platforms is more profound than you may think, because it influences
the structure of the economy. It helps make possible both small
and independent businesses. Countries like England that saw
the rise of an independent farmer class in the seventeenth and
eighteenth centuries depended on town marketplaces (records
indicate more than eight hundred in England alone) where they
could sell agricultural surplus.[4] In the software industry, thanks to
platformization over the 1970s, it became possible for developers to write "to the platform" as opposed to building their own
computers.

Making possible extreme specialization and small producers
has ripple effects on economic and class structure. Platforms help
determine who can participate in the economy. What we really
are speaking of here is the link between open platforms and economic freedom.

Fourth Problem: The Promotion of Innovation

When Netflix began operations in the 1990s, it was entirely
dependent on the postal system, a form of public platform,
through which it mailed DVDs[*] (in red envelopes) to people's
homes. The postal system wasn't originally designed to carry
video, but its design was flexible enough that it worked anyhow.

---

* DVD stands for "digital video disc," a disc-shaped form of digital storage widely used
from the 1990s to the 2000s to hold films and other video content.

As this example suggests, another less obvious but profound feature of a successful platform is that it can facilitate the evolution of products or services—otherwise known as innovation. What does that mean? It means that a well-designed and well-functioning platform can support new versions of a given product and service, as opposed to locking the offering in time. This is a complex point, but an important one, and one that is key to understanding the importance of policy principles like net neutrality.

One easily underappreciated feature of a city street or square is its "future-proof" nature. The ancient medieval squares in places like Marrakesh and Siena are still places where stuff is sold every day, even if the stuff itself has changed over the last five hundred years. The city square is a fairly future-proof technology, as is the shopping street, even in an age of online shopping. For example, the same physical store that once sold buggy whips and typewriters might now repair damaged phones and sell bubble tea. The same infrastructure supports evolving uses. Jane Jacobs, the great prophet of the city economy, made much of this fact in her books, including *The Death and Life of Great American Cities* and *The Nature of Economies*. As she pointed out, the great advantage of a city architecture is its ability to support change in uses, and Jacobs correctly predicted the persistence of the city itself, unlike those who predicted the rise of the Internet would mean the death of the city.

This point becomes more complex when we speak of technological platforms. In the design of platforms, it takes a good design to avoid obsolescence. There is a significant danger of building a platform that becomes forgotten or itself becomes a barrier to innovation because it is too narrowly designed for the specific uses of a certain time, such as the Japanese mobile phones of the 1990s.

A classic example of this problem comes from France. In the 1980s, the French government introduced a home networking system known as the "Minitel," a combined network and home terminal system. In its own way, the Minitel was very advanced and quite impressive. French citizens got a free little computer terminal in their home that could do many things, like display the weather and news. It even offered a rather basic version of online shopping. The Minitel's broad distribution—consisting of its nine million terminals—put France ahead of other countries. In some ways, the French got there first. They already had something like our contemporary Internet and the Web much before the rest of the world.

Unfortunately, unless you are French, you probably haven't heard of the Minitel, because as a technological platform, it had an important flaw: it was designed and optimized for the technologies of the 1980s and 1990s. It was designed to work with text, for example, as opposed to graphics. Things that worked for the Minitel only worked for the Minitel. It remained stuck in the early 1990s, unable to adapt to change.

In contrast, the Internet, whose basic design in the 1970s actually preceded the Minitel, had a much more open and adaptable design, which has proven to be one that has lasted through generations of change.* It managed to evolve from the support of simple text-based applications in the 1970s (like email), to the user forums in the 1980s, the websites in the 1990s, streaming video in the 2000s, and more recently, things like artificially intelligent chatbots. Not unlike the electric grid, it has remained constant while the products and services on top of it have changed.

Underlying the Internet and the city square is the same deceptively simple but actually brilliant idea, which is to be as neutral as possible between uses. There is a kind of impartiality built into a shopping street: it doesn't care if the stores on it sell top hats for men or fruity yogurt drinks; it is optimized for neither. A booth at the farmers market can sell fruit in the summer, squash in the autumn, and so on. The temptation to optimize technological infrastructure to fit the needs of the day is hard to resist, but it brings the risk of obsolescence.

WHAT IS OLD AND WHAT IS NEW

Given this sizable log pile of economic effects, it is hopefully obvious by now why platforms of various kinds have been at the foun-

---

* The core TCP/IP protocol, designed by Vint Cerf and Robert Kahn, dates to 1973–74.

dation of most prosperous civilizations. Like a kind of economic wonder drug, platforms are linked with economic opportunity for diverse producers, the opportunities for farmers, entrepreneurship, and innovation. It is also not so surprising that there is no "inventor" of the platform, in the same way that there is no single inventor of the bridge, road, or other parts of economic infrastructure. It is perhaps most accurate to say that the history of platforms has, until recently, been closely tied with the history of cities themselves.

These are what might be best described as positive sides to platforms, including tech platforms. It helps explain why there was so much excitement in the early 2000s about the broad flourishing that the Internet economy was going to make possible. But there are significant differences between the historic open platforms and our current generation. Most of all, the ownership and ambitions are different. Unlike, say, a public town square, the tech platforms are private, profit-seeking corporations. They are also generally unregulated, unlike, say, commodity and stock markets.

It would seem weird to describe an old-time town square or shopping mall as having grand ambitions. But today's platforms have an acute self-awareness of their own value and power. They are not satisfied with serving as mere catalysts. Ever since Bill Gates fully demonstrated the ability of a tech platform to dominate its ecosystem and extract most of its value, the platforms have sought to rule the economies that they serve. In the chapters to come, we shall see how that played out, starting with the very first computing platform worthy of the name.

CHAPTER 2

PLATFORMIZATION

THE FIRST COMPUTING PLATFORM

In the 1960s, the United States had a new and growing computing industry, centered on the sale of giant "mainframes" owned by corporations and universities. But the idea that software could be a product—something you sold—was not at all a familiar one. The word "software" itself was new, coined by a statistician named John Tukey,[1] who had a knack for naming things.* In 1958, he wrote that "the 'software' comprising the carefully planned interpretive routines, compilers, and other aspects of automative programming are at least as important to the modern electronic calculator as its 'hardware' of tubes, transistors, wires, tapes and the like."[2] This usage, in an engineering journal, is widely believed to be the first in-print instance of the word "software" and hence the first naming of what would become one of the largest U.S. industries of the late twentieth and early twenty-first centuries. But in the 1960s, software was just something that

---

* He was also possibly the first to use the word "bit" in computing (short for "binary digit"), though some sources suggest Claude Shannon used it in the same year.

programmers at giant companies like IBM wrote to make the machines work.

By the late 1970s and early 1980s, there had been a change so great as to make computing unrecognizable. There were now not just a few, but thousands of software companies engaged in all sorts of niches and sub-niches. Commercial software development was no longer confined to a few firms, mainly on the East Coast, but was now happening everywhere, in places like California and later Texas and Washington State. The industry that would become one of the world's most valuable and impactful— worth trillions today—had begun its long expansion.

What happened is "platformization." By that I mean the creation, within an existing industry, of a platform that made a new class of businesses and products possible. The computing industry became platformized, and all those new companies were writing "to the platform." That created, in effect, an industry where none existed before.

It's hard to overstate the importance of the platformization of computing. Over the early 1980s, software began growing explosively, with annual growth of over 40 percent in real terms. According to the Bureau of Economic Analysis, software grew from $17 billion to $190 billion in value over twenty years.[3] It became part of a larger industry valued at $1.9 trillion of U.S. value-added GDP by the 2020s, a number that is an understatement of its full value. The birth of software as an industry permanently changed the economies of Northern California, Washington State, Texas, and other areas and along the way dramatically changed the U.S. workforce and what it does.

The platformization of software was important, but neither accidental nor something that was destined by some kind of natural law. Instead, the birth of the American software industry is a story of a push and pull between private industry and public government—and a story of unusual boldness and courage on both sides.

Let us return to the early 1960s, when IBM was the largest and most advanced computing company in America and the world.

IBM was in many ways the grandfather of the American comput-ing industry. Yet if imagined as a grandfather, IBM was like one of those elderly relatives who turns out to have been a bit weirder than you ever realized. The firm grew to prominence under its first leader, Thomas Watson Sr., who ran the company not unlike a very large cult. His picture and quotes adorned the walls; his employees sang songs glorifying him and the company; the dress code—a dark suit and tie—was strict. In exchange, Watson Sr. did treat his employees well, and he loved nothing better than holding a big tent-camp revival for his people.

Entering the 1950s, IBM was not a computer company but rather a manufacturer of electronic accounting equipment. As the decade began, and as electronic computing started to show commercial potential, IBM seemed likely to miss the future by sticking with its punch cards. Large and successful companies often find it hard to adapt to new technologies (think Kodak and the advent of digital photography), given the risk of cannibaliz-ing their existing business. Watson Sr. by that time had become almost a caricature of the aging leader who failed to adapt to changing times. In a famous but probably apocryphal anecdote, he was said to have estimated a world market for computers of "maybe five." In the words of historians Ralph Watson McEl-venny and Marc Wortman: "The senior Watson fundamentally did not believe computers would serve business purposes."

It was fortunate for IBM that Tom Watson Sr. had a son (Tom Watson Jr.) who, after goofing around for most of his youth, man-aged to recover and make it into the executive ranks. Junior had a better sense of the future than Senior and managed to wrest con-trol of the firm from his father, after a complex drama resembling the 2020s television show *Succession* but with a different ending.

Watson Jr. sensed that the punch card's day was coming to an end. He quickly ordered IBM's engineers to turn their energies to developing fully electronic machines; the company debuted its first line of computers in 1953, the IBM 700 series, which ran on vacuum tubes. IBM's preexisting relationships with America's corporate world were an asset, and by 1961 IBM was growing faster than any company ever had outside of wartime. But its success drew rivals, and over the 1960s IBM attracted significant competitors both at home and abroad. There were new firms like Control Data Corporation who were building supercomputers that outperformed IBM's best. And from overseas a threat came from Japan, where the Japanese government was actively organizing a national champion—a Toyota of computing—to challenge the American heavyweight.

By the mid-1960s, Watson Jr. and his chief engineers felt they had to make a bold move for IBM to stay ahead. The radical idea was the creation of a single set of standards to which all IBM products would work, and a single operating system to unite them all. IBM would build the first "general purpose" computer, named the System/360. In this venture, we see the beginnings of the first true computing platform that would change everything.

It helps to understand that at the time, computers were a bit more like appliances: sold for specific purposes, such as record-keeping or accounting, or used by scientists to solve highly complex data operations. Each model was programmed to be its own, nonstandard product that didn't work well with others. Many computing systems were custom-built for the needs of individual companies.

By creating an entirely new system, IBM was making a high-stakes bet; its revenue as of 1962 was about $2.5 billion, and the development of the new computer line would require double that amount.[4] It was a "bet the company" kind of investment. And it is a testament to its ambition and execution that IBM managed to pull it off.

The technical and strategic genius in the System/360 can be examined a little more carefully. Today we take for granted a rough interoperability of most computers and electronics. But in the 1960s, the IBM System/360 allowed a business for the first time to buy machines with confidence that they would actually work together. And the idea of a standardized operating system—a piece of software that sat on top of the hardware and told it what to do—was particularly important for what was to follow.

The System/360 was not just an engineering feat but also a brilliant business strategy, for it took an already dominant position and successfully built it into a monopoly. Only IBM's software and devices worked with IBM, making the buyer of the System/360 a customer for life, reliant on IBM for all their needs. Its wild success made it, in the words of historians McElvenny and Wortman, the "'thinking machine' at the heart of virtually every large organization for more than two decades."[5]

But IBM's growing monopoly, however lucrative for IBM, began to attract a different kind of attention. Complaints from competitors and others drew the attention of the federal government; more specifically, the American antitrust authorities, who began their own investigation.

Most people with a passing familiarity with American history know that the country has long abhorred monopoly. Not only did the United States invent anti-monopoly laws (antitrust), but it also had Theodore Roosevelt, the original "trustbuster," who, in the 1900s, began the movement that would break up some of the largest monopolies in history. What fewer people realize is just how important those laws were to the postwar economy, or how aggressive the Justice Department was during that period, under both Republicans and Democrats. This ended up having great effects on the development of the first tech platforms and the American economy more broadly.

Here's a brief introduction to the antitrust laws, first enacted in 1890 and intended to serve as an antidote to monopoly and its attendant evils. They were passed during a time when the rise of monopoly was a great popular concern. As Supreme Court Justice John Marshall Harlan recounted in 1911, "the conviction was universal that the country was in real danger from another kind of slavery sought to be fastened on the American people, namely, the slavery that would result from aggregations of capital in the hands of a few individuals and corporations controlling, for their own profit and advantage exclusively, the entire business of the country." Or, as Senator John Sherman, sponsor of the Sherman Antitrust Act, put it: "If the concerted powers of [a monopoly trust] are entrusted to a single man, it is a kingly prerogative, inconsistent with our form of government, and should be subject to the strong resistance of the State and national authorities."[6] The word "trust" meant monopoly, so the laws are better understood as "anti-monopoly" laws.

The laws are not self-executing or automatic: they require prosecution through complaints filed in court. The dependence on enforcement and open-ended language has given latitude for different administrations to fill in their own preferences and priorities. In the hands of Theodore Roosevelt, the law was a cudgel with which he broke up the "bad trusts" (abusive monopolies) like Standard Oil, whose power Roosevelt saw as a threat to democracy. But other administrations, like those of Calvin Coolidge and George W. Bush, preferred a much lighter touch—so light, in fact, that the cudgel became more like a feather. For much of the last forty years—from the 1980s through the late 2010s—the law has often been enforced in a meek, cautious fashion, following the dictates of a framework (the so-called Chicago School of Antitrust) that recommended government action rarely and preferably never.

Back in the 1950s and 1960s, the anti-monopoly enforcers were of a different and much tougher mindset. They were closer in disposition to Theodore Roosevelt and tended to see the stakes of anti-monopoly as transcending mere economics and spilling into questions of democracy and political destiny. Influenced by the recent experience of the Second World War, American officials believed that fascism and corporate monopoly were linked. They feared that excessive corporate power would bleed into fascism or contribute to a communist uprising. Famed antitrust enforcer Thurman Arnold blamed German monopolies for helping Hitler rise to power: "Germany became organized to such an extent that a Fuehrer was inevitable; had it not been Hitler it would have been someone else."[7] Here's how Senator Estes Kefauver put things in 1950: "I am not an alarmist, but the history of what has taken place in other nations where mergers and concentrations have placed economic control in the hands of a very few people is too clear to pass over easily. A point is eventually reached, and we are rapidly reaching that point in this country, where the public steps in to take over. [. . .] It either results in a Fascist state or the nationalization of industries and thereafter a Socialist or Communist state."[8]

Over the 1950s and 1960s, a succession of American officials translated these ideas into action. They took aim at mergers and industries that they deemed too concentrated for the health of the economy and the republic. That did not fully prevent firms from growing—to take an obvious example, General Motors and the other automobile manufacturers grew into giants during this period. But antitrust officials did file big lawsuits against leading American firms, including Alcoa, the aluminum monopolist, AT&T, the Bell monopoly, and IBM. The lawsuit against AT&T was particularly important: AT&T, by a 1956 court order, was required to stay out of computing indefinitely and license its transistor patent to anyone for free.

Over the late 1960s, the Justice Department turned its attention to IBM. The firm held a sustained monopoly over mainframe computing and was generating complaints about its hardball tactics. There was evidence of IBM throwing its weight around—in particular, stemming from its nasty reaction to the challenge thrown down by a Minnesota start-up, the Control Data Corporation (CDC) over the 1960s.

Control Data was a start-up composed of a group of former military code breakers. The resident genius was a man named Seymour Cray, a master of computer hardware design whose only apparent life ambition was to build the fastest computer the world had ever seen. Cray's first design for Control Data was one of the first computers based entirely, not just partially, on transistors (not vacuum tubes). He then spent four years designing what he considered his masterpiece, the world's first supercomputer: the CDC 6600.

When it debuted in 1964, the CDC 6600 was a landmark that blew past IBM's fastest machines. It was, in fact, three times as fast as IBM's best and sold for $7 million per machine, instead of the $13 million that IBM wanted for a slower unit. It is not often that a smaller company so completely outmatches its much larger competitor, and the launch of the CDC 6600 alarmed IBM leadership. CEO Thomas Watson Jr. wrote an internal memo on the topic:

> Last week, Control Data had a press conference dur-
> ing which they officially announced the 6600 system. I
> understand that in the laboratory developing the sys-
> tem there are only 34 people including the janitor. Of
> these, fourteen are engineers and four are programmers
> and only one person has a PhD. [. . .] Contrasting this
> modest effort with our vast development activities, I fail
> to understand why we have lost our industry leadership
> position by letting someone else offer the world's most
> powerful computer.[9]

IBM's technological response was to commission some two hundred engineers to build a machine faster than the CDC 6600. But
that effort went wrong somehow and failed to deliver a sellable
machine compatible with IBM's newer machines. When it comes
to innovation, bigger is not always better.

That failure seemed to have led IBM, if unable to beat its
opponent in terms of performance, to rely on its size, power,
and tricks of the trade. For despite its cheery corporate culture,
IBM and its management did have a darker side. Tom Watson
Sr. may have been an inspiring force, but he was also convicted
of criminal antitrust violations in 1913.[*] The Justice Department
had already investigated and sued IBM twice for violations of the
antitrust law—in 1932 and 1952. And while not strictly speaking
a business offense, IBM allowed itself over the 1930s to become
closely involved with the Nazi regime; Germany was its most
profitable foreign market during that period. IBM, of course, was
hardly the only American firm to make money selling to Nazi
Germany. But Watson Sr. would be one of the few Americans
personally presented with a medal by Adolf Hitler for service to
the Third Reich. (Watson Sr. did later return the medal and dis-
own the relationship.)

* While working at a different firm, the National Cash Register Company (NCR).

Control Data filed a lawsuit in the 1960s alleging that IBM salesmen were approaching potential customers for CDC's computers and using IBM's size and power to scare them off. An IBM salesman might, for example, threaten to cut off a customer from IBM's full line of products if it bought a CDC supercomputer. IBM also told customers they should wait for a new machine— the IBM/360S, which would be faster than anything Control Data was making and also sell at an extraordinary low price. The machine, it turned out, did not actually exist, and IBM knew it would be unable to deliver it on time or make any profit at the prices it was promising customers. Nonetheless, it seemed worth the sacrifice to slow down the rise of IBM's most dangerous competitor.

Beyond IBM's treatment of Control Data (and similar tactics against other rivals), the Justice Department also believed that IBM was suppressing the market for independent software. That's because, as we've learned, it was IBM's practice to sell software together with computers in one all-inclusive bundle. There was no option to buy software or get a computer without it: buying IBM meant buying it all. With the buyers' needs met, there was little room left for independent software to make much headway.*

Some may read this and think that IBM's tactics were fair, part of the give-and-take of market competition. Cutting off customers would surely only hurt IBM in the long run. As for the vaporware (nonexistent products announced to hurt competitors), that was bad manners; but as Robert Bork, the famed advocate of Chicago School antitrust, once said, the law should not be a code of etiquette.[10] Announcing vaporware might have been a form of lying, but also a smart business strategy for a dominant firm.

It is true that business is not a dinner party, and there's a difference between etiquette, morality, and what we might take as fierce competition. But the key difference here is the presence of monopoly power. The law holds the monopolist to a different standard than the ordinary company, because the effects are

---

* IBM, in technical jargon, was "tying" its monopoly in hardware to its software products, foreclosing independent developers. The best evidence of an effect (at the time) was the lack of any real software industry, despite a potential made obvious by later developments.

different. That which is done by a corner store, or a group of rivals locked in combat, has much different industrial consequences than acts undertaken by a firm that is acting to defend and maintain a monopoly. The former is competition; the latter impedes it, and also allows the monopolist to maintain their hold on power. If the monopolist is allowed to do what any firm does, the result can be an indefinite monopolization of industry.*

In 1968, the Justice Department presented its concerns to IBM, and inside the firm, the legal team assessed the risk. Burke Marshall, IBM's general counsel at the time, analyzed the relevant cases and concluded that under the antitrust law as it then stood, the software-hardware arrangement would be impossible to defend. Marshall saw bundling "as a glaring violation of antitrust law," and suggested that if forced to defend the tie, IBM "would lose."[11]

Watson Jr., the CEO, had survived a previous antitrust attack in the early 1950s by settling, and doing so had in some ways made him and the firm stronger. In contrast, his father had been convicted trying to fight the Justice Department, and Watson Jr. didn't want to repeat that mistake. Hoping for another quick settlement, Watson Jr. made the decision to begin the process of separating IBM's software offerings from its hardware offerings in late 1968.

That may not seem like much, but there are times that seemingly small decisions can change history, and this was an example of just such a decision. IBM began selling its software separately on June 23, 1969, on what some later called the "Independence Day" for the software industry.[12] Seventeen computer applications were made independently available for sale, as opposed to being packaged with the computer. That, coupled with the System/360, was the final step that completed the platformization of the software industry. It would take some years for independent software to get going. But as one historian later put it, the events of that day "effectively created the modern software industry."[13]

---

* In the specific case of IBM, the question of recidivism also appears to have influenced the Department of Justice. Justice and IBM, as we've said, had a history and Justice seemed to see the firm as incorrigible.

With software now separated from hardware, with the effective opening of the System/360, the basic elements were in place for an explosion in software entrepreneurship. In retrospect—given the impact on computing—it seems a brilliant stroke. But at the time it was deeply counterintuitive to those who thought IBM was just being punished for its success.

ANTI-MONOPOLY AS INDUSTRIAL POLICY

In its attack on IBM over the 1970s, the United States was swimming in a direction different from other nations. During that same period, most countries were doing everything they could to *help* their "national" computer companies. Most countries saw computing as akin to aerospace—that is, a symbol of technological pride and national security, an industry that needed and deserved government aid and protection.

That was certainly the case in Europe. The French government poured money into Bull (Compagnie Des Machines Bull) and its advanced Gamma 60 computer. The British had International Computers Limited (ICL), formed by a state-mandated merger. Italy's engineers had built the very elegant Olivetti Elea, and the Soviet Union, playing catch-up, created the EC ЭBM, a state-produced clone of IBM's System/360.

But the most organized effort to take on IBM came from Japan. By the 1960s, Japanese engineering was roughly on par with its Western counterparts, and an attention to detail and process would soon establish automotive firms like Toyota and Honda as world-beaters. At the beginning of the 1960s, the Japanese Ministry of International Trade and Industry—the brain center of Japanese industrial policy—identified computing as a priority for the national economy and decided to advance a national strategy to promote Japanese computing.

While the American firms fought one another, the ministry thought Japanese manufacturers would do better working together as a team. It supervised the formation of an industry-wide partnership named the Japanese Electric Computer Co. (JECC), comprised of Fujitsu, Hitachi, NEC, Toshiba, Mitsubishi, and Oki—every major computing company in the nation. Backed by generous state loans, the JECC divided up computing research and development among the firms, working together to challenge IBM and the rest of the world. As Marie Anchordoguy details in *Computers, Inc.*, "by avoiding redundant research and gaining scales of production, [MITI thought] Japan would be better positioned to stand up to IBM."[14]

Because it faced the rise of competitors from abroad, the logical thing might have been for the U.S. government to say something like: "IBM is an American success story. Let's help them out." Or maybe to just say "let's leave things alone." The latter is laissez-faire; the former is a form of industrial policy, namely the "national champion" policy being pursued in Japan and Europe at the time.

The United States, through the Justice Department, took neither of these options. It neither helped IBM, nor left it alone. Instead, as we've seen, it took a third option: challenging IBM and seeking a full breakup of the company.

A simplistic view might suggest that the Europeans and Japanese were engaged in industrial policy while the United States favored antitrust. But in retrospect, it is clear that the United States was just practicing a different kind of industrial policy. As opposed to subsidizing its largest computing firm, it was forcing it to back off and create room for competitors. By a rough analogy to sports, it was calling defensive fouls to give the other teams a chance. Or, by an analogy to gardening, it was hacking limbs off the biggest tree, hoping that something new would grow given a chance to catch some sunshine.

The officials at the Justice Department didn't talk this way; it is not the language of law enforcement. They said that American law prohibits the abuse of monopoly power, and they were simply engaged in enforcing the law as written. But it now seems obvious that they were practicing industrial policy, just using the stick instead of the carrot.

In any event, the bet paid off. Yes, it would take some years for the software industry to find its feet. But gradually, more and more firms were born to write "for the platform." They didn't have to do a deal with IBM, or know anyone: they just had to follow the rules. Figures like the young Bill Gates, Steve Jobs, Larry Ellison, and others all started small companies that either built to a software platform (an operating system), or would in time create their own platform.

The effects on the labor market for talent should not be understated. The most ambitious and talented software programmers of the 1970s did not end up as mere functionaries in the IBM empire, but instead started their own firms. Platformization creates opportunity. And it also changed the regional calculus—a more open market brought the West Coast, Texas, and Massachusetts into a software and computing sector previously dominated by New York and New Jersey. The operating-system platform itself was such a successful model that it was copied for other computing systems, such as the minicomputers of the 1970s (mainly forgotten systems like the DEC computer), and was at the core of the Apple personal computer when it launched in 1976. By that time, it had become standard, and the software explosion was underway, yielding the creation of a multitrillion-dollar industry.

How do we know the platformization of software mattered? Was the explosion inevitable? A telling and important fact is that those comparably wealthy, advanced, and technologically savvy nations—Britain, Italy, France, and Japan, for example—did not undergo the same experience as the United States, and did not benefit from any such explosion or growth of a new industry. It is true that the United States held the most talent and capital, giving it a natural advantage. But that was true of other industries, like the automotive industry, where the United States held an early dominance, only to lose it to other nations. By 1984, "the United States utterly dominated the world market for software products," supplying 95 percent of the market.[15] And while challenged, the United States still pretty much dominates the software world decades later.

It is instructive to compare what happened in American computing and software to other industries and nations. The Japanese approach worked—at first. It successfully grew the Japanese computing industry into a significant world power. But in retrospect, the longer-term downsides are also obvious. The Japanese ministry envisioned an integrated model of computing and never forced any platformization of software. It therefore never witnessed the development of an independent software industry. Outside of computer gaming, Japanese tech has never quite overcome that.

Things got worse in the 1980s, when Japan doubled down on its centralized planned approach to the future of computing. Beginning in 1982, the ministry invested in the so-called Fifth Generation computing project, which was designed to leapfrog the West with a new type of supercomputer. The program was premised on the simple idea that faster is better and that the nation with the fastest computers would be sure to win the race to the future. But, of course, the future is hard to predict. Bigger is better is often the right bet, but not always. In the 1970s, few would have thought that the future would belong to tiny and cheap personal computers coupled with independent software, but that's what happened. Sometimes a little anarchy can be a useful thing, and the Japanese approach left little room for organic growth.

The comparison with other American industries is also instructive. The American aerospace industry was, like American computing, an early leader, dominated by three firms: Boeing, McDonnell Douglas, and Lockheed Martin. But American policy was nearly the exact opposite of that in computing. The government, largely through defense contracting and pressure on U.S. airlines, took the national champion approach. Eventually Boeing merged with McDonnell Douglas, emerging as the one American company. While there has been some improvement and innovation in aerospace, the difference between the passenger airplanes of the 1970s and those we now fly in has been incremental—certainly nothing like the difference between today's computers and those from the 1970s.

Boeing, which has struggled through the 2020s, is what computing would look like if the United States had decided to support and save IBM and AT&T—an overgrown mess. As George Romney of American Motors put it at the time, "Like boxing champions who lack suitable opponents, companies [deprived of rivals] become soft and flabby."[16]

Zooming ahead to our present, we can see that the United States is again pursuing antitrust as an industrial policy by filing complaints against Google, Facebook, Amazon, and the other major platforms. The calculus, roughly, is this: indeed, these are impressive firms that have launched impressive products. But they cannot be allowed to merely wield their existing power and money to hold on to dominance. Google, in its 2023–24 monopolization trial, was caught spending over $20 billion per year to ensure its search product would remain the industry default, and to keep Apple out of the market. Facebook spent over $20 billion to prevent Instagram and WhatsApp from emerging as rivals. The phrase for this is "buying your way out of competition."

Antitrust enforcement by challenging the monopolist can serve as a key tool of economic rebalancing. Its remedies can be used to open platforms and target excessive aggregations of economic power. It is, in that sense, an essential element of an alternative to both pure capitalism and communism.

THE OPEN INTERNET AND THE FIRST NET NEUTRALITY RULE

The other great platform of the late twentieth century was—duh—the Internet. The story of the American tech revolution of the late twentieth century was, simply put, a story of two open platforms—the operating system and the Internet. Yet while the story of the Internet revolution has been told many times (including in my own book *The Master Switch*), it is essential to understand the roles that platformization played in creating the Internet's golden age.

The Internet was conceived of at roughly the same time as IBM's System/360 and in a similar spirit. Its government funders envisioned the creation of what they jokingly called an "Intergalactic network"[17] and a "network of networks,"[18] meant to interconnect all the other computer networks in the world. The technical breakthrough that made it possible was the theory of packet networking and the TCP/IP protocol, designed in the early 1970s. But from the beginning, the Internet's design distributed power and resources to those at the "ends" of the network, that is, those on the network, as opposed to the owner of the network itself. It was, in its way, a modest design that relied on the passive virtues of connection and empowering others.

The credit for the Internet's design goes to the scientists and engineers who collectively came up with it. But there is more to the story. For it to work, the Internet had to run on something, and that something—the physical wires—was the AT&T telephone network. In other words, for the Internet to reach its potential, and to actually reach people, it was going to have to do so on the physical network of the Bell phone system. Unfortunately, Bell happened to have a pretty low view of the Internet and the technologies it embodied. [*] That is why it is easy to forget that without a challenge to AT&T's power, it is doubtful that the mass Internet would have taken off in the United States at all.

Let's return to the early 1970s. At that point, AT&T was the largest company on the planet, with over a million employees. After becoming the uncontested monopolist of telephone communications in the early 1920s, it had wired the country and created an impressive long-distance system that was a world leader. Bell was a believer in its "One System" philosophy—which stood for the idea that one company should own and run everything, and that everything would be better that way. It was an unabashed monopolist (and, as a company, something of a control freak), but preferred to see itself more as an enlightened despot, the wise and all-powerful guardian of American telecommunications.

AT&T's brain trust did not have a high regard for technologies invented outside of the company, and took a particularly dim view of the experimental computer networks being set up by universities and the Defense Department. The underlying technology, packet networking, struck AT&T officials as "preposterous."[19] "Their attitude," said Paul Baran, one of the inventors of the Internet protocols, "was that they knew everything and nobody outside the Bell System knew anything."[20]

The Internet as we know it could easily have remained a

---

[*] The federal government actually offered AT&T the opportunity to take over the early Internet in the 1970s, but the company declined. Janet Abbate, *Inventing the Internet* (Cambridge, MA: MIT Press, 1999).

slightly obscure network used by research universities to transmit large amounts of data. Just as with the opening of the computing platform, it took a mixture of business bravery and structural government action to platformize what we now know as the commercial Internet. It took the debut of the first net neutrality law—the ancestor to the laws that require fair carriage of content on the Internet.

In the 1970s, every home (and business) had a telephone, and a line provided by AT&T. That is just the way it was. As computer networking became more sophisticated, a new kind of business— now largely lost to history—began offering remote computing services over the telephone lines. With names like Tymshare, National CSS, CompuServe, and Dial Data, their business model was to offer a very, very early version of what we now call "the cloud." These were tiny, itty-bitty firms. Had AT&T simply said, "let it be," and played nice, things might have been different. But the firm's reaction was so intense to what it took as an invasion of its prerogatives, that it earned itself a date with the federal government—both with its trustbusters and its anti-monopoly regulators throughout the 1970s. Which ended in, among other things, the breakup of the company.

But in some ways even more important for platformization was the promulgation of the first net neutrality rules by the Federal Communications Commission (FCC) in the early and mid-1970s. Going by an obscure name—"the computer inquiries"—the FCC wrote rules that forced AT&T to allow others to run a business "on top of" the telephone network. If CompuServe wanted to let its customers dial up and reach their services, AT&T had to let them. And it had to do so in a manner that was both "permissionless" (i.e., you didn't need to ask AT&T) and at a "zero-price." The regulators of the 1970s were not wimpy. Perhaps surprisingly to modern ears, the Nixon regulators were some of the toughest. They mandated rules requiring AT&T to allow others to run their businesses over AT&T's pipes, so long as they paid their bills. It is an idea that is simultaneously radical and natural at the same time.

With these rules, AT&T's network would be an explosively

powerful kind of platform—a truly public platform operated by a private entity, and a resource for any builder.

The first to build "to" the network were the sellers of answering machines, modems, and other devices, not to mention alternative "long-distance" providers.[*] The second were so-called online services companies like CompuServe and what would become America Online (AOL). When AT&T resisted the net neutrality rules over the 1970s, the antitrust division backed up the FCC, bringing a complaint that eventually yielded the 1984 breakup of AT&T into eight smaller firms. That development, like the IBM case, further weakened the monopoly's ability to slow down competitors or new products, especially when AT&T was banned by the court from involvement in "electronic publishing," leaving the market to newcomers. In combination and in time, those newcomers led services that became the popular Internet of the 1990s. It was a development that thrust the United States back into a position of technological leadership and led to the development of some of the most valuable companies on the planet.

Like forcing IBM to open software, net neutrality was a kind of industrial policy that restrained the monopolist. By doing so at the right time and place, it helped spur economic growth worth a hard-to-measure amount—surely hundreds of billions in additional growth through the 1990s and early 2000s. It is hard to precisely measure the economic impact of all the companies that grew on the Internet—though it says something that most of the major tech firms, with the exception of Apple and Microsoft, got their start as websites.

Might this have happened anyhow if AT&T had stayed in charge of the network? If it hadn't been forced to adhere to net neutrality rules? One can never know for sure, but once again the international comparisons are telling. It is telling that the main rivals to the United States in the 1980s and 1990s, Japan and Europe, declined to impose similar controls or break up their

---

[*] In previous times, "long-distance" telephone service referred to making phone calls between cities as opposed to within a city—the former was billed at a higher price. The distinction between local and long-distance services evaporated in the 2010s.

telephone monopolists. And they ended up following very different paths, mainly centered on cellular phones that were an extension of the main monopoly over telephones. Ultimately the sleek smartphone was not created by any phone company. Really a small computer with the ability to make telephone calls, it ended up being developed in the United States by the computer and software industries.

If there is another lesson to take from both stories, it is that neither the private nor the public sector has a monopoly on vision or brains. IBM and AT&T were impressive, massive creatures that built important landmarks. But they also overgrew and sought to stifle succeeding generations. The government, meanwhile, had no particularly insightful vision of technology's future, but it did bet on using its own power to countervail and restrain monopolistic power in the interests of giving others a chance. Those bets took a long time to pay off, but they paid off in spectacular fashion, yielding a return to American technological supremacy and an age of great optimism to which we now turn.

CHAPTER 3

THE GOLDEN AGE OF TECH OPTIMISM

The extent of tech optimism over the late 1990s and early 2000s is hard to overstate. Tim Berners-Lee announced that "the goal of the Web is to serve humanity. We build it now so that those who come to it later will be able to create things that we cannot ourselves imagine." The Internet was new and fresh; millions were "surfing the web," and thousands were playing around with their websites and web-logs (aka blogs). For some, it was an enthusiasm fortified by hopes of making a fortune. Investor and venture capitalist John Doerr called the dot-com boom of the late 1990s "the largest legal creation of wealth in the history of the planet."[1] For others, the Internet was offering a kind of deliverance on the countercultural ideals of the 1960s and 1970s. If the human potential movement had seen personal liberation as the goal, the Internet seemed to offer a tool for unlocking the latent creativity and passion within every soul.

Clay Shirky, author and technology pundit, captured the tech-optimistic mood of the mid-2000s with a slogan: "Here comes everybody."[2] Anyone could have their own political soapbox, or blog, their own recording studio, their own video channel. In our jaded times, overloaded with opinion—much of it virulent—

and the spread of influencers, we can forget how revolutionary it really felt for anyone, potentially, to reach the world.

The small-is-beautiful spirit also bled into commercial and economic matters. *An Army of Davids*, published in 2006 by professor and early blogger Glenn Reynolds (the "Instapundit"), described the "little guy" theory of the 2000s most cogently.[3] Reynolds believed that thanks to technological changes, the future would belong to smaller economic units: "[A]s technology moves toward smaller, faster, and cheaper approaches to many jobs, we're likely to see an army of Davids [small or individualized businesses] taking the place of those slow, shuffling Goliaths." These developments, Reynolds predicted, "will represent a dramatic reversal of recent history, toward more cottage industry, more small enterprises and ventures. [. . .] We're likely to see a movement from impersonal, imposed means to an end to a more individualized, grassroots way of doing things."

It followed from this that the age of the corporate dinosaur was over; that the giant firm was facing an extinction as certain as that which faced the brontosaurus. The large media companies like Time-Warner were slow-moving and run by fumbling fools, bewildered by the Web, desperately spending money to remain relevant. Microsoft, the most powerful private platform, had just been humiliated by the U.S. Justice Department. The future belonged to the streamlined companies, the mammals who would run circles around the dinosaurs.

Some went further, believing industrial organization itself was obsolete, and that groups of spontaneously self-organizing users were the future of production. Yale scholar Yochai Benkler was among the intellectual leaders in this respect. He observed the startling success of Wikipedia (a volunteer operation) and the open-source Linux operating system, also built by volunteers. He argued that we were witnessing the rise of an entirely new mode of production, which he labeled "commons-based peer production." As he wrote, "its central characteristic is that groups of individuals successfully collaborate on large-scale projects following a diverse cluster of motivational drives and social signals, rather than either market prices or managerial commands."[4]

If there was one point of agreement, it was that decentralization would rule the twenty-first century. Dozens of thought leaders had predicted a decentralized future in which the "goliaths" didn't stand a chance. But at the risk of stating the obvious, things didn't quite go as predicted. To say it again: only rarely have so confident a set of predictions been so wrong.[5]

What went wrong? The mistake, as we've learned, was a failure to truly understand platform power—that is, the interests and abilities of the growing private platform owners. The flourishing of the 1990s through 2000s was built on the back of public platforms—equivalents to technological town squares, which had been funded by the government or otherwise operated under intense government oversight. The Internet, meanwhile, was built on a combination of infrastructure either directly funded by the government (like the ARPANET and NSFNET) or by firms like Microsoft or the phone companies, who were under federal oversight.

Somehow, many assumed that the new and rising platforms—places like Google and Amazon—would also behave as public-spirited town squares that existed to help others, almost like corporate charities. The firms, for their part, tended to encourage that view. As Google's cofounder Larry Page put it in 2004: "We want to get you out of Google and to the right place as fast as possible." There was also Google's famous code of conduct: "Don't be evil."

Let's spend a moment on Google, bearer of the famous slogan.[6] It may be hard for younger readers to understand how widely the firm was seen as a beneficent entity. Jeffrey Jarvis in 2009 wrote an entire book titled *What Would Google Do?* that treated the firm as a kind of oracle of altruism. His book taught "the wisdom of Google's ways" and preached "a set of rules to live and do business by."[7] Peter Thiel similarly lauded Google, in its monopoly form, as a uniquely enlightened firm. Google, he wrote, has "wider latitude to care about its workers, its products, and its impact on the wider world."[8]

That was the 2000s. But by the 2010s, something had changed. Over the 2010s, the main tech firms had established a new playbook for maximizing use of their platform power. Gone were the paeans to small-is-beautiful and the transformation of the human existence. In its place was a strategy that extracted from dependent businesses and harvested the time and data of the masses. So was the idealistic talk of the 2000s all just a ruse, "sentiments for suckers," meant for investors and employees who wanted to feel good about themselves?

I personally don't think firms like Google were sinister operations just playing nice in the 1990s and 2000s while secretly harboring dark plans for the future. For some time—much of the 2000s—Google arguably pulled it off. Its products were both good *and* enormously profitable, and at that point it had not yet done anything particularly evil. The problem came later—when the mission and money began to collide.

The banal explanation is that—with the exception of Wikipedia*—the high-minded platforms of the 2000s all chose to become ordinary Delaware corporations answerable to shareholders and Wall Street analysts. Google and friends talked a good game but selected the same corporate structure as firms like ExxonMobil, Pfizer, and Walmart, a structure that since the 1980s has put shareholder welfare as the value above all others. Google believed that even though it was subjecting itself to public corporate duties, it could nonetheless hold on to its soul through a sheer act of will.

That's evident from the 2004 letter that Larry Page and Sergey Brin wrote to investors, styled "an owner's manual for Google's Shareholders."[9] It opened with these lines: "Google is not a conventional company. We do not intend to become one." It warned investors that it was dedicated to long-term value creation, not short-term returns, and that it intended to treat its employees well, providing "unusual benefits" such as "meals free of charge, doctors and washing machines." It mentioned "don't be evil," and a desire to be "a company that does good things for the world even if we forgo some short-term gains." The firm "aspire[s] to make Google an institution that makes the world a better place."

---

* Jimmy Wales, the founder of Wikipedia, deserves credit for resisting easy wealth (based on Wikipedia's traffic) and making the organization into a nonprofit. No one is accusing Wikipedia of trying to monopolize markets, hurt children, or erode democracy.

Looking back, the letter exudes a confidence bordering on delusion that Google would be the one company in history uniquely capable of resisting the forces that tend to drive corporations away from any higher purpose. To take just one example: the letter blithely presumes that both advertisers and users can be served without real compromise, when of course they have opposing interests.[10*] The founders thought they could ignore the warnings in Scripture about the impossibility of serving two masters, but they were wrong.

Over time, structure beats out good intentions. Like an endless stream wearing away rock, the pressure for Google to produce more revenue eroded its youthful dedication to a higher purpose. Today the search engine is profitable but so clogged and choked by advertisements as to make a mockery of putting user interests first. The advertising side of the business does everything it can to squeeze out every cent. In 2018, reflecting what it had become, Google moved its "don't be evil" motto from the front to the end of its employee code of conduct.

For the platforms, everything seems to have changed roughly over the years 2012 and 2013. If I had to choose one symbolic day, it would be June 11, 2013, for the reasons that follow.

Our story begins in the year 2006, at the height of the excitement surrounding spontaneously self-organizing projects. That year, an Israeli programmer named Ehud Shabtai founded a website named FreeMap Israel. Strongly influenced by the success of crowd-sharing projects like Wikipedia, Shabtai thought a community-driven online mapping service might make a lot of sense. Unlike other mapping programs, much of the content was contributed by the users of the map itself. FreeMap met with success and moved into mobile. As an app, it renamed itself Waze.

At that stage, Waze was earnestly pursuing Yochai Benkler's vision of a community-driven challenger to more commercial alternatives, including an older firm named MapQuest and a

---

* The tension between advertiser and user interests should be self-evident; it is described extensively in *The Attention Merchants*.

newer map program run by Google. As Waze grew, it began to monetize the business and became a serious rival to Google Maps. The success seemed to portend a showdown between two models: one more commercial and centralized, run by a major firm; the other a decentralized approach centered on peer contributions.

But just as the competition began to heat up—as the contestants were stepping into the ring—the contest was called off. In June 2013, Google announced it was buying Waze for $1.3 billion.[11] It was as if the Yankees, facing the Oakland A's in the World Series, had announced they would be buying their opponent.

Given the existence of antitrust laws whose project is to prevent monopoly, it might be very natural to wonder about the deal's legality. The text of the relevant law on mergers bars any acquisition whose effect is to "substantially lessen competition, or tend to create a monopoly." On its face, Google–Waze certainly looked like it would "tend to create a monopoly," given that for the average commuter Google and Waze were the two main choices in online mapping services. So the question became: What would the Federal Trade Commission—the agency tasked with reviewing the merger—do?

Google, taking advantage of a loophole, did not formally notify the federal government, but the Federal Trade Commission took a look anyhow. After a brief investigation, it elected to do nothing, and for many years there was some mystery surrounding this decision. It was well known that a rosy view of Silicon Valley prevailed at the time, not to mention a taste for noninterventionist microeconomics. But the merger was so blatantly and obviously anticompetitive—so evidently the creation of a monopoly, that even by the standards of the 2010s it was hard to know how the lawyers had justified the decision, even to themselves.

It was only many years later, after a few drinks with staff attorneys, that I got the answer. The relevant head of the mergers division decided he wanted to clear the deal based on the following theory. Waze was an app that told you "how you get there." Google Maps, in contrast, was an app that told you "where you are." Hence, by that logic, the firms weren't actually competitors at all. It takes many years of training to reach conclusions this absurd.

Here's why the acquisition of Waze marked the end of the era when the Internet was seen as the great equalizer. The idea of self-organizing little producers beating big guys presumed a fair playing field. But the contest between Google and Waze was won not by any contest of models but by paying off one of the fighters. Instead of some kind of twenty-first-century contest, Google used nineteenth-century industrial buyout techniques. The past was back—with a vengeance. But would it reach the most decentralized of all markets, the thousands of new e-commerce sellers born on Amazon?

CHAPTER 4

FROM ENABLEMENT TO EXTRACTION— THE STORY OF THE AMAZON MARKETPLACE

If there is one thing that the tech pundits in the 2000s were certain of, it was that the future of American retail would belong to the little guys. Here, again, is pundit Jeff Jarvis:

> There won't be a single new retail behemoth to battle Wal-Mart like Japanese monsters in Tokyo Bay. Instead, Wal-Mart and other big chains are getting nipped at their heels by a million tiny competitors—a half a million of them on eBay alone. In 2007 eBay sold $59.4 billion in merchandise from 547,000 online stores. [. . .] In 2007 eBay beat the sales of America's largest department-store chain, Federated (aka Macy's), with revenues of $26.3 billion in 853 stores.[1]

The future is hard to predict, so while this prediction was wrong, it was at least wrong in interesting ways. It was, of course, Amazon that became the ascendant power in retail over the 2010s, a behemoth rising not out of the Tokyo Bay but Puget Sound. But, to give Jarvis credit, Amazon didn't emerge in the same way as a more integrated firm like Sears or Walmart. What

Amazon did was not to ignore the open platform, but rather to become the platform. How that happened provides a key to understanding the platform power playbook of the 2010s.

As everyone knows but may have forgotten, Amazon was once just an online bookstore. It opened its doors to the public in 1995 with a certain bluster, calling itself the "world's largest bookstore."[2] At the time, it was not really a platform: it sourced and sold the books itself. (One basic difference between a platform and a normal store is that the latter selects and assumes ownership of the products being sold.) Amazon's basic idea at the time was to take advantage of being a warehouse that could ship books anywhere.

Amazon first became a platform—a place for others to sell stuff—in the year 2000. The "Amazon Marketplace" started small and was initially something of a gimmick. It opened in November of that year as a place for used bookstores to sell their books right next to new ones, through a link. That placement outraged publishers (of new books) who accused Amazon of "directly harming authors" by offering an easy way to buy a used book for half the price of a new one.[3] But Amazon ignored the criticisms and, as the decade proceeded, slowly began opening its marketplace to more and more sellers, product line by product line.

As the Amazon Marketplace gained momentum, Amazon leadership began realizing a few things that now seem obvious. First and foremost, that there was a great deal of money to be made being a marketplace for others to sell on. Over time it would become obvious that there was much *more* money to be made that way than by being a store. The Amazon Marketplace generates more transactional value than Amazon direct—$480 billion in sales in 2023, constituting some 83.5 percent of total platform sales (Amazon's direct sales in 2023 were roughly $95 billion).[4] Second, it became clear that a good search engine was key to matchmaking (Amazon developed a search engine, A9, which for a while was a competitor to Google search). Finally, that convenience and reliability were the keys to catalyzing transactions, not just for buyers but for sellers as well.

That last point may sound boring, but it is the key to Amazon's success. Over the long grind of retail competition, sellers are attracted to whatever makes it easiest to fulfill customer orders. To meet that need, in 2006, the Amazon Marketplace hit on the winning formula with a key commercial innovation: offering a full suite of "order fulfillment" services, including storage, packaging, and shipping assistance to sellers, for a reasonable fee. "You send products to Amazon, and we take care of the rest," advertised Amazon—a promise irresistible to small sellers struggling with logistics. What Amazon was doing was something platforms can do—reduce your need to be a fully integrated business.

The prices for sellers, meanwhile, were very reasonable at the beginning (the 2000s). The handling fee was as low as $0.50 per item, plus $0.40 per pound, plus a storage fee of $0.45 per cubic foot, per month.[5] It was such a good deal for sellers that fulfilling orders was not a strong moneymaking proposition for Amazon for many years.

But third-party order fulfillment was a powerful aid to growth, and with fulfillment, Amazon jumped far ahead of eBay, once the largest marketplace, which failed to offer convenient services to help sellers fulfill orders. (It would only launch such services in 2019, way too late.) eBay sellers needed to store and package their own stuff and ship it. That's a model that, to state the obvious, does not scale particularly well—that is, it works fine for sending out a few items a day but cannot cope with significant demand. Some eBay sellers even managed to use Amazon to fulfill orders during this period.

By the 2010s, Marketplace had become the easiest and most straightforward way for a small business with a good product to bring it to market. The proverbial designer of a better mousetrap might not find it easy to get on the shelves at the local retail store or know how to operate their own website, but Amazon had room for everyone.

For a spell, it worked well for pretty much everyone. By 2014, Amazon's revenue was at $89 billion.[6] eBay, which had seemed a giant when Amazon was a baby, got stuck at $18 billion.[7] And in 2014, the cost to sellers of selling on Amazon was reasonable, averaging out at about 19 percent of revenue (traditional retail is 50 percent).[8] Sellers were happy, Amazon's stock was rising, and it seemed that the win-win promise of the Internet was being delivered. It was the dream of the 1990s realized: the magic platform in the sky that helps everyone sell to everyone else.

Consumers, for the first time, had access to more products
than ever before, and reviews to boot, which provided more
information than packaging. Producers had a way to find buyers,
and everyone had the advantages of convenient shipping. It was,
in a sense, an economist's dream: a near-frictionless platform of
unlimited size and complete information, connecting buyers and
sellers who might otherwise have never found each other.

These attractions induced many to take the plunge and start
their own businesses during the 2010s. Take the story of Doug
Mrdeza, a barber from Michigan who began selling surplus hair
products on Amazon in 2014. His first offering (a specialized
pomade) sold out, so he began selling more products. He gradually established a company, Top Shelf Brands, centered on the
Amazon Marketplace, with a line of men's hair products. Things
were going very well. As he later reflected, "It was like living
the dream" of small business success.[9] He hired more than forty
employees—people looking for work after the Great Recession—
and was bringing in some $10 million in revenue a year. "It was
thriving, for sure," he said, "we were all in."[10]

Lindsay Windham of Charleston, South Carolina, was
another who took the plunge. She is a designer who used a Kickstarter campaign in 2011 to fund her business, named Distil
Union. Its specialty was "to simplify life by creating problem-
solving products that are a delight to use,"[11] like those credit card
holders that attach to a phone, or alarm clocks that won't fall off
a bedside table. She and her partner gained traction on the Amazon Marketplace over the 2010s and made a business of it.

All was going well for sellers like Windham and Mrdeza. But
then came the late 2010s, when Amazon turned to what would
best be termed its "extraction" phase.

Let's back up a little and take a look at the Amazon Marketplace's growth strategy. By the late 2010s, Amazon had achieved
a secure dominance on the seller side through a two-pronged
approach. The first was a strategy of growth at any cost, including a willingness to lose money in the process—particularly in
building out new services. Contrary to mythology, for most of

its history Amazon wasn't losing billions a year (that was Uber), but more or less breaking even—making or losing hundreds of millions. (The unexpected profitability of its Web services division helped.) A second strategy was buying rivals, including competitors like AbeBooks (used books, acquired in 2008), Zappos (online shoe sales, acquired in 2009), and Diapers.com (acquired in 2010). The federal government, in the depths of the antitrust winter, approved all these mergers without comment, reasoning that Amazon was still a small player in the larger world of retail. At the same time, as we shall detail, Amazon also cleverly subsidized its buying side (users) with enticements like free shipping for an annual fee (Amazon Prime, which debuted in 2005) and a variety of entertainment products beginning in 2012. As we've seen, subsidizing one side can be a key strategy for platforms—akin to the old practice of holding a "ladies' night" to attract a crowd.

For many sellers, as Amazon reached a certain size, alternatives became largely implausible. Doug Mrdeza, the barber selling pomade, estimated by the late 2010s that 90 percent of his revenue was coming from Amazon.[12] With more than 100 million paying Prime members in the United States by 2020 (168 million by 2022),[13] there was realistically no choice for a seller who was already hooked on Amazon sales. With its market power established, Amazon began ratcheting up its fees to sellers. It steadily increased the monthly seller fee (the mirror image of Amazon Prime) to $480 per year (or $39.99 per month).[14] Then it began to ratchet up other fees to reach about 30 percent per sale.

More damage to seller margins came from the rise of a new kind of fee, the advertising fee.* Amazon didn't call it a fee but portrayed its "sponsored result" advertising as an opportunity to get preferred placement in search. As with many things Amazon, the feature had been around in some form for a long time (since

---

* Like many tech founders, Jeff Bezos has always viewed advertising with disdain—at least for his own products. As he put it, "Advertising is the price you pay for having an unremarkable product or service." But as a tool of extraction from Amazon's sellers, it proved lucrative.

2012), but in the late 2010s Amazon took steps to make spending on ads effectively mandatory.

Here's how it worked. No one buys your stuff if they can't find it. Amazon's search had at one point been relatively "straight," that is, keyed to things like high ratings, low prices, and relevance. However, Amazon, beginning in the late 2010s, began making most of the visible results depend on payment—so-called sponsored results. Those who didn't pay were demoted. Sellers soon realized advertising was not an opportunity but an obligation. In other words, the advertising program was more of a "pay up or suffer the consequences" story—the Tony Soprano school of business.

There is more to it than that, because Amazon's scheme cleverly put sellers in a competition for the top spots—a tournament. Whoever was willing to pay Amazon the most got the best chance at a sale but at the greatest expense. The program quickly became one of Amazon's most lucrative profit centers. From the early 2010s, when advertising brought in less than a billion,[15] revenue began to explode, reaching $10 billion by 2018,[16] $20 billion by 2020, and an extraordinary $56.2 billion in 2024.[17]

Let's back up and examine Amazon's advertising business (if "advertising" is indeed the right word). At $56 billion, it is about double the advertising revenue of the entire newspaper industry, and not just in the United States but globally ($28.44 billion in 2023).[18] It is not only large but also highly profitable, given the lack of costs on Amazon's side. Astute observers, like Benedict Evans, believe that ads are actually Amazon's most profitable business line, more profitable than the Web services.[19] And what, exactly, does that money go toward? The money sellers and consumers are shelling out doesn't make the platform better in any obvious way; the ads are not necessarily a signal of quality. Instead, they make search results more confusing and difficult to navigate. In short, sellers (and users) are spending nearly $56 billion to make the buying experience worse. It is a pure example of valueless wealth extraction.

All these fee increases were making Amazon a worse place for sellers. Recall that Amazon's fees in 2014 totaled less than

20 percent of the selling price.[20] By 2023, fees had become less predictable, but when averaged amounted to over 50 percent of the sales price of the average product.[21] In some cases, as Marketplace Pulse relates, "A few sellers showed paying 60 percent and even 70 percent of their revenue to Amazon in fees," not quite realizing until the end of the year how thin margins had become.[22] Marketplace, at first a seller's dream, had become for many a kind of trap. As on Pleasure Island in *Pinocchio*, the sellers who were lured in by candy and good times found themselves hooked and unable to leave.

None of this is to suggest that there was no value in what Amazon provided and continues to provide sellers. It is still the world's largest marketplace, and at this point, many sellers face a choice between Amazon or much smaller alternatives. As a place for third-party sales, the Marketplace has no real competition in the United States (Walmart, which surpassed eBay as the second-largest marketplace, has 6.4 percent of online retail, an order of magnitude smaller).[23] By 2024, the Marketplace had gone from a break-even operation to one that was earning the firm profits of $60 billion a year (including the advertising profits), more than its profitable Web services (approximately $35 billion per year).[24] Its annual fee revenue from third-party sellers in 2023 was $185 billion, a fourteen-fold increase from 2014. Marketplace had clearly become Amazon's leading cash cow and one of the greatest examples of economic extraction the world has ever seen.

Beyond fees, independent sellers' lives weren't made any better by the habit that Amazon developed of selling its own, in-house products in competition with breakout products. For example, a small firm named Peak Design, which makes outdoor products, met success with an "Everyday Sling"—a kind of handbag targeted to men and photographers, priced at $99, which debuted in 2017.[25] In 2020, Amazon debuted its own "Amazon Basics Everyday Sling" at $35, a strikingly similar product. Amazon can also elevate itself in its own search results, making a mockery of the auction for placement.

There's also the matter of Amazon's spying on its own sellers.

In July 2019, I was sitting at the same table as Amazon's lawyer at a congressional hearing when he said, under oath: "We don't use individual seller data directly to compete."[26] But this turned out to be untrue, based on admissions by former employees later revealed by *The Wall Street Journal*. Amazon's staff have long used data harvested from sellers to decide which products to compete with.

Take the Fortem trunk organizer, a product sold by a four-person operation out of Brooklyn that found success in the late 2010s. (The trunk organizer is a kind of divided open container that keeps a car trunk organized.) Amazon decided to launch its own version in 2019, but only after carefully reviewing detailed information on Fortem's sales, profit margins, advertising spend, and other data. As a former Amazon employee explained, "We would work backwards in terms of the pricing." In other words, they were looking for a margin to exploit.[27]

What were the combined effects of these changes? This much is clear: they make independent sellers less profitable and Amazon more profitable. Amazon, once a break-even operation, has become highly lucrative. The result has been a straightforward transfer of income and wealth, from David to Goliath. It is a classic case of pre-distribution in favor of the already wealthy.

For the barber Doug Mrdeza, the growing fees eventually cut too far into margins to continue paying his employees. By 2019, he was forced to fire all but five of his employees. He tried expanding to eBay and his own site, but more than 90 percent of revenue was coming from Amazon through its fee structure. If you "actually add up all the ways Amazon nickels and dimes you [. . .] you can't make money,"[28] he told the Institute for Self-Reliance. In 2022, he declared bankruptcy and laid off the remainder of his employees.

Other businesses are hanging on, and it isn't impossible to run a business on Amazon, but it has become harder. Sellers describe a love-hate relationship: "If we could make similar sales elsewhere, we would, but we can't," wrote one seller on an Amazon seller forum. "Every 'improvement' Amazon makes is to extract as much revenue from your sales as possible."[29] While many small American businesses have been squeezed out, Amazon's marketplace is quite workable for Chinese businesses who are willing to store goods in the United States while handling everything else in China.

Amazon remains an essential and unavoidable marketplace—the main street or city square for an entire class of small businesses. The bad part is that unlike the old city squares, it has its own interests in profit maximization. It sucks revenue and profit from independent businesses, maintaining a margin that favors itself.

With these changes something else has disappeared: the prospect of Amazon's platform serving as a catalyst of significant independent wealth creation, or the rebalancing of economic power. Early Amazon held out a real prospect of changing class dynamics in the United States, by enriching an entrepreneurial sector of small businesses across the nation. But the creation of a class of independent businesses means less if they are dependent upon a far larger business. They become a dependent class, and at its worst, can end up in a near-feudal relationship with the mother ship.

The story of Amazon's 2010s rise to essentiality and gradual squeeze of its sellers represented the new playbook in the platform strategy. Summarized, it suggested the following steps:

1. Establish the platform as essential to transactions, by lowering effective costs and prices to both buyers and sellers.

2. Eliminate rivals through acquisition or subsidized pricing.

3. Clone the most successful dependent businesses.

4. Seal the exits for buyers and sellers—with both carrots and sticks.

5. Extract wealth by raising prices and fees for buyers and sellers, increasing ad load, and mining data and attention.

Each of these steps has been followed by the major platforms in different ways. And a key ingredient in this recipe—a matter also misunderstood in the early 2000s—was scale and its effective usage.

CHAPTER 5

SCALE AS A WEAPON

If getting Amazon wrong represented a misunderstanding of the extractive potential of the platform, maybe the single largest intellectual error committed by the optimists of the 2000s was a gross underestimate of the lasting relevance of scale. Small, unfortunately, would not become the new big.

What exactly is scale? Scale is a word with many meanings, but in business and economic jargon it refers to the relative size of a business's facilities, as well as to the advantages that come with producing or selling at high volume. If you own a farm that raises a few chickens or sells homemade jams, you're engaged in what is called "artisan" production. But in business lingo, if you take that same farm and buy and raise a thousand chickens, you've now "scaled the business."

Scaling a business—rapidly increasing the volume of production—can have dramatic effects on an industry. It usually reduces the number of firms competing, and in some cases yields a monopoly.* Reduced to its essentials, the Industrial Revolution

---

* Monopoly is common when the advantages of scale are linked with another principle: "network effects," in which a business gains an advantage by having more customers or

can be described as a giant scaling project, in which scale manufacturing overcame artisanal methods of production.

The effects of scale are particularly obvious in manufacturing, especially of commodities. Take the example of flour. Over the 2010s there was an uptick in businesses relying on artisanal methods of flour production, usually involving an old-school stone grinder. The costs of such small-scale production are less than they used to be, but individual artisans have trouble getting prices below $4 or $5 per pound. In contrast, the industrial methods of flour production—giant plants, fields of wheat—have managed to drive the price of producing flour down to less than 40 cents per pound. You must really like artisan flour to be willing to buy it.

A classic, and in some ways the original example of scaling was the mechanization of textile production in England from the 1780s through the mid-nineteenth century. That was made possible by the invention of power looms and spinning machines, which dramatically lowered production costs. The upside was cheaper clothing, but the textile story is also a cautionary tale of scale's broader effects. The rapid displacement of artisan labor by machines led to terrible outcomes for the working population, including the rise of the textile mill and its brutal working conditions, which persist in sweatshops around the world. Eventually workers recovered, but there was much suffering along the way.

As these examples suggest, scale has a history closely linked with traditional large manufacturing and network businesses. But there are other types of business that do not react so well to a change in scale. Beer brewed in bulk may be cheaper but is lacking in the flavor department. If a restaurant owner opens too many branches with too little supervision, it can easily go downhill. As food critic Pete Wells once asked in a scathing takedown of celebrity chef Guy Fieri (who opened far too many restaurants in the 2010s): "Have you eaten at your new restaurant in Times Square?"[1]

---

users. The classic example is the telephone network, which is more valuable the more people you can reach on it, which was once used to justify AT&T's monopoly.

Services—the by-products of skilled labor—are particularly hard to scale. Take a talented plumber—he or she can try to fix more burst pipes but will run into the fact that there are only twenty-four hours in a day. As the plumber example shows, there are cases where smaller-scale operations can beat out the big guys. In the 2000s it seemed unclear how the new, folky Web businesses would react to scale—whether they'd gain or be ruined. If the typical Web business of the 2000s was the charming personal blog, the tiny start-up, or the maker of customized wooden cutting boards, it wasn't obvious what would happen.

We've already said that some, like Seth Godin (*Small Is the New Big*), thought the advantage would belong to the smaller, nimbler businesses. But there were others who always suspected the opposite: that big, scaled businesses would come to rule the Internet. The two books that made that prediction were *Blitzscaling* by Reid Hoffman and Chris Yeh and *Zero to One* by Peter Thiel, one of the PayPal founders. To the dismay of many, they were right.

In *Blitzscaling*, Hoffman and Yeh argued that everything about the twenty-first century greatly favored the rise of scaled platform businesses and that businesses faced a choice: scale or die. They defined "blitzscaling" as "the science and art of rapidly building out a company to serve a large and usually global market, with the goal of becoming the first mover at scale."[2] They also opined that "software has a natural affinity with blitzscaling, because the marginal costs of serving any size market are virtually zero."[3]

Thiel took these ideas one step further, encouraging every tech business to pursue monopoly. The obvious reason to do so was to make money. Billions, if you did it right. But Thiel also sought higher ground and argued—in an echo of nineteenth-century social Darwinism—that monopoly was not just profitable but an evolution toward a more beneficent way of being. As he wrote in *Zero to One*, monopoly "is the condition of every successful business."[4] Inverting Tolstoy's comment about happy families, he said, "All happy companies are different: each one earns a monopoly by solving a unique problem. All failed companies are the same: they failed to escape competition."

The two main advantages of getting big are reduced costs of production (efficiencies), and better capacity to bully others (or to resist bullying). But which matters more? Well, one thing we know is that the efficiencies of scale run out once you reach a certain size. You may be able to raise chickens for less when it is one thousand at a time instead of five at a time. But if you're raising a million chickens, there are no further gains and instead the beginning of losses of efficiency.

As the chicken example suggests, it is clearly the case that at some point, the "diseconomies of scale" start to creep in, especially as time goes on—this is the "Curse of Bigness." Corporate bloat is real, and large companies can suffer from organizational problems, managers who feud or develop their own agendas, or just the sheer impossibility of coherently organizing so many functions. As the corporate raider T. Boone Pickens once put it, "It's unusual to find a large corporation that's efficient. I know about economies of scale and all the other advantages that are supposed to come with size. But when you get an inside look, it's easy to see how inefficient big business really is."[5]

What's left after a firm has grown too big may not be any great efficiency but just the capacity to bully. And on this point Hoffman and Yeh were quite candid: a major function of scale, they wrote, was to serve as a weapon—as the warfare-themed title of the book suggests. They described a business strategy based loosely on the blitzkrieg, a military strategy used by the German army in World War II to overwhelm the Polish, French, Dutch, and Belgian armies in rapid succession. "The theory of the blitzkrieg," said Hoffman in an interview, "was that if you carried only what you absolutely needed, you could move very, very fast, surprise your enemies, and win."[6]

Hoffman and Yeh argued that the fundamental reason to invest in massive scale at money-losing speeds was to reduce "the risk of competition." As they put it, "Your goal is not to beat the competition. Your goal is to break free of competition entirely." The best means to do that was to "achieve a critical mass that confers a lasting competitive advantage."[7] By this, they meant entrenching the firm's presence in consumers' lives, so that switching would become unlikely or impossible. As Hoffman put it in an interview, "You want to scale faster than your competitors because the first to reach customers may own them, and the advantages of scale may lead you to a winner-takes-most position."[8]

For his part, Thiel went for a loftier defense of the pursuit of power and monopoly, borrowing from Friedrich Nietzsche and René Girard. The merely competitive firm was Nietzsche's last man—"incurably mediocre."[9] Great firms avoided imitation and instead pursued a "deserved" monopoly—with products so special and desired that they had no natural competitor. And ultimately this corporate Übermensch would have more room to inhabit a beneficent greatness: "wider latitude to care about its workers, its products, and its impact on the wider world."[10]

Blitzscaling and *Zero to One* ended up capturing the real spirit of the 2010s. Over that decade, every major platform raced to acquire scale-based monopoly and become entrenched in the lives of millions. More servers, more employees, more data, and more computing power. And thanks to Thiel and other self-congratulatory prophets, the platform leaders could also feel satisfied that doing so was not just self-interested but also the right thing to do.

Even if we grant that firms like Facebook and Google did have great products and the right timing, and did indeed take "deserved" monopolies by 2012 or so—what then? Time reaches us all and has a way of obsoleting even the best products—as the story of Facebook suggests.

Facebook was clearly the dominant social network of the 2000s, with stronger code and better design than its rivals. But by the early 2010s, it was beginning to show signs of age and look dated. It worked well only on the desktop, not mobile devices, and was not particularly good with photos. There was plenty of room for the rise of a social media platform that was mobile and photo first. Along came Instagram in the early 2010s—a start-up that went from nothing to nearly 40 million users in the space of two years.[11] So, what did Facebook do? Afraid of the prospect of a competition it could lose, it bought its most dangerous rival for a billion dollars.

Even great firms that build monopolies don't always find

them easy to hold on to, and it is in the "holding on" part that the darker side of corporate practice emerges. It is like in politics, where a young populist reformer may sweep into power on the strength of good ideas, only to become, after some time, the kind of leader who would feed his political opponents to crocodiles, in some cases literally. For big tech the key strategy was not mere internal growth but the practice of "denying scale" to any emerging competitor.

Over the 2010s, several strategies were used to deny scale to any nascent rivals. One strategy involved paying to prevent rivals from gaining scale, a tactic practiced most often by Google, which was spending more than $26 billion annually by the 2020s to keep its competitors locked out of distribution channels.[12] Another tactic, practiced by Amazon, involved preventing dependent businesses from selling for less elsewhere. The simplest and most effective method, however, was old school: the buyout. The monopolist could hold on to its position by buying any company that might potentially rise to become a challenger, no matter how small or insignificant—to put out even the merest spark, lest it become a dangerous fire.

That strategic logic led to some high-profile purchases, such as Facebook's buying out of Instagram and WhatsApp for more than $20 billion and Google's acquisition of Waze. But far away from the headlines, the strategy meant further billions spent on the acquisition of hundreds of smaller firms, most of which then faded into nothingness. One study of the acquisitions conducted by Facebook, Microsoft, Google, and Amazon from 2007 to 2018 revealed that they collectively acquired over one thousand firms.[13]

Many of the firms acquired over the 2010s were not, perhaps, destined for greatness. But the occasional rise of unlikely firms like Twitter showed that you could never be so sure. Weird ideas sometimes pan out. Publicly, the companies described the acquisitions as forms of hiring, or "acqui-hires." That said, they also managed to stamp out the threat of anyone with the wherewithal to start their own company and put out a product.

Of course, the would-be challengers were enriched and not unhappy; tens of millions of dollars have a way of cushioning the death of any dream. But some would come to regret becoming a minor functionary of a much larger empire. As Waze founder Noam Bardin put it, "When you decide to sell a company, you need to be honest with yourself that this is the end of your era."[14]

The story of Waze is telling. The founders were drawn in by the payout and the promise that they'd remain independent within Google. Waze would fall into place as a kind of solid alternative to Google Maps, but it did not become any serious competitive threat or develop its own ecosystem. In 2022, Google ended Waze's independence by combining the staff working at Waze and Maps. As Bardin said, "Looking back, we could have probably grown faster and much more efficiently had we stayed independent."[15]

The longer history of corporate gigantism also reveals serious macroeconomic risks. For a giant firm might be broken and inefficient inside—quite bad at what it does. Yet, like a literal dinosaur, it can still possess enough weigh to stomp on any arising rival and scare off others. It may persist, not due to any real excellence, but because it has become too large to dislodge and too good at protecting itself.

Multiplied a few times, any country risks becoming a land of stagnant giants. Lest that seem far-fetched, over its history the United States has had plenty of tech companies that grew to suffer the curse of bigness, firms that were high-tech darlings in their day, including Xerox, Kodak, IBM, General Motors, and many others. Other giants, like Intel and Boeing, both once considered to be at the pinnacle, have suffered a litany of size- and management-related problems and sunk into lengthy declines.

There is little doubt that blitzscaling worked for the platforms of the 2010s. But whether it worked for the country is a different question. That's why if industrial scale were a drug, it would be a stimulant. Powerful and addictive, scale upends the industries and lives of firms. It can be useful to make things happen, move the needle, and bring an economy out of a stupor. It can create a form of mania at the level of firm and scale. As the saying often misattributed to Stalin goes, "Quantity has a quality all of its own."

But just as actual stimulants lead to crashes, so it is on the industrial scale. The cycle of excessive growth followed by collapse can do lasting damage to any industry and any nation, leaving behind regions devastated and slow to recover. The book *Blitzscaling* tells only half the story. It does not tell firms how to deal with the hangover of getting too big, too fast, nor tell a country how to deal with the decline and collapse of oversized firms.

CHAPTER 6

THE GREAT HARVEST

In the "here comes everybody" period of the early 2000s, billions of people signed up for the platforms and became free to publish their photos, opinions, and videos to a broader world. It was widely assumed that this would revolutionize the media landscape and empower a creative class everywhere.

It is true that the last twenty years have remade media. Creative types for twenty years now have been able to easily publish songs or videos, and anyone can start a blog or Substack to spout views on one's subject of choice. It has also gotten easier to argue online about a baseball team or find groups online catering to any manner of unusual interest, such as the Reddit group that discusses alien autopsies (r/AlienBodies). It was a group of new platforms—especially the social media platforms—that gave the little guys a place to do their thing.

But these were not uncommercial activities—they were, in the lingo, "time on site." And the projected triumph of the creative class was a bust. For the millions of "Davids" who flocked to the Web over the 2000s were not challenging the new "Goliaths" in any meaningful way. Rather, they became, in large part, Goliath's unpaid or underpaid servants. They joined Goliath's army and made him rich.

The book that best captured the new dynamic was written by independent filmmaker Astra Taylor and named *The People's Platform: Taking Back Power and Culture in the Digital Age*. She pointed out, in 2014, that the platforms had not, in fact, done much to improve the lot of the "middle-class" creator. In her view, putting out a viral video does not equate to a career in the creative industries. Instead, the Internet was wiping out a cultural middle class to replace it with new "cultural plantations" ruled over by West Coast aggregators.[1]

The new social media platforms like YouTube, Facebook, and Twitter made it easier to do things that took some work to do directly on the Web, such as creating a website or sharing photos. They also aggregated it all, creating an attraction for others. But that never translated, economically, into the rise of a new creative class holding significant wealth (with the exception of influencers, discussed below).

Of course, for most people, a Twitter account or a Facebook page wasn't something they took on as a commercial undertaking. Most people did not make money, nor expect to make money, as amateur bloggers or posters of Instagram content. Telling the world what you had for breakfast is not something most expect to profit from. We should not discount the meaning and joy that many have experienced from, say, drawing their own comic for a small audience, or writing a blog or tweets for fun.

But as Taylor pointed out, there were some people who were hoping to make money in the arts—even have a career—and yet their fortunes got worse, not better. However noncommercial the users' motives may have been, the owners of the platform were less charity minded. As time went on, the social media platforms slowly turned the dials and extracted more and more from their users. Platforms, to keep profits increasing, needed to drive "engagement," which they did by making them increasingly cluttered, manipulative, and unhealthy—the process my old pal Cory Doctorow calls "enshittification."[2] This was the direct by-product of serving two masters: 1) users, and 2) advertisers, which is the model of the so-called attention merchant.

What was happening here, in the aggregate, was an economic exchange, but one that was highly tilted. Many users of social media were and are like tenants who spend hundreds of hours renovating their landlords' homes. The users, en masse, were handing over human attention, predictive data, and whatever they might happen to build. "The information economy that we are currently building doesn't really embrace capitalism," wrote technologist Jaron Lanier, "but rather a new form of feudalism."[3]

The users of social media, like Instagram, did two things at once, and both are rather amazing in retrospect. First, they created an attraction for others like them, bringing in people's time and attention, both of which could be advertised to. The second was allowing the collection of so much data—what scholar Salomé Viljoen calls "predictive data"—as to allow sites to predict the behavior of entire populations.[4] This was both a means to make money (through resale to data brokers and advertising), and also, independently, a source of economic power.

It is also true that some people—who came to be called influencers—managed to convert their social media standing into actual jobs. One source suggested that those who managed to accumulate over 50,000 followers could pull in an income of between $40,000 to $100,000 per year.[5] Those with giant followings could make millions a year. The social media platforms, in that sense, created at least one new economic class—one group, other than the platforms themselves, that was prospering in the new economy.

Yet the influencer was plainly a laboring class, as opposed to one with ownership over any productive asset. For the job of an influencer requires constant effort to harvest attention. This has made burnout and mental health problems the black lung of the influencer industry, as countless examples attest.

Take the story of Lee Tilghman, a bubbly and pleasant young woman from Connecticut who found success as "Lee from America," an Instagram wellness and diet influencer. Over the 2010s, she built up a following with her healthy recipes (smoothie bowls), yoga, and other lifestyle tips. She also attracted sponsors and advertisers as she reached over 400,000 followers. At the height of her popularity, Tilghman could command some $20,000 for a single Instagram post advertising one product or another.[6] She was earning lots of money, in effect, to live a healthy life—what could be wrong with that?

But her physical health and mental health were moving in opposite directions. The constant pressure to post content became a heavy weight—the "digital treadmill," which Tilghman later called "performing your life for content."[7] It can be hard—exhausting—to constantly come up with fresh content. As former TikTok star Jack Innanen once said, the experience is like "tapping a keg that's been empty for a year."[8] Suffering from stress and the recurrence of an eating disorder, Tilghman scaled back and eventually quit. She later came to revel in the relative freedom of a normal, predictable nine-to-five job in which work stops at the end of the day. As she told *The New York Times:* "When you're an influencer, then you have chains on."[9]

Influencers describe other challenges that come with a career driven by views and clicks. Consider the saga of Elle Mills, a YouTube star from Ottawa, who began posting videos in 2010 as a twelve-year-old. By the late 2010s, her short videos about home life found success and by 2018 she had reached over a million followers and was earning significant money.[10] But the Internet fame took its toll and Mills wrote a particularly insightful piece on what it means to live life as a quantified brand.[11] Success, she wrote, requires that you "make yourself into a product and figure out how to sell that product." Given that success is measured in views, the numbers make it clear when you've done well. "The numbers feel like an adrenaline shot to your self-esteem," she went on. "The validation is an addicting high, but its lows hit just as hard." For her, the real stress began once she had gained a massive audience. Mills "was constantly terrified of losing my audience and the validation that came with it. My self-worth had become so intertwined with my career that maintaining it genuinely felt life-or-death." Like many before and since, she burned out and quit YouTube in 2022.

While highly visible and culturally important, the influencer and other social media industries also remain relatively small potatoes in the big picture of marketing and commerce. These were not yeoman farmers who would arise to challenge feudal lords and establish a kind of influencer middle class. With their prominence, incomes, and seemingly easy lives, influencers might appear to be the Internet's ruling class. But this is an illusion—they need to work for every dollar, have limited economic security, and do not own the means of production, putting them in the same boat as the rest of us.

PART II

THE BUSINESS OF HERDING

In 2017, Scott Galloway, the popular podcaster and professor of marketing, was ready to announce the winners. In a book titled *The Four* he wrote that Amazon, Facebook, Google, and Apple had left everyone behind in the tech industry, based on their market valuation, user bases, and general influence. That same year, the American TV personality Jim Cramer began using the acronym FAANG for Facebook, Apple, Amazon, Netflix, and Google based on their stock performance.[1] Goldman Sachs coined the acronym GAFAM to refer to the same group plus Microsoft.[2]

The emergence of these groupings by the mid-2010s signified a turning point. The main tech platforms had emerged as the dominant tool for harnessing the economic and social energies made possible by an interconnected nation and world. Two were in new markets (search and social networking); one was in retail, and there was Apple, which was building an entire ecosystem of living. They'd made it big and bought off some dangerous competitors. But as they approached the 2020s, each of the majors faced the same big question: Having made it, how to stay there?

In this part of the book we shall investigate how the platforms, having gained economic power, have managed to hold on to it. We have already discussed one method—the purchase of competitors and using scale as a weapon—but the full story leads us beyond the basics of platform economics into some more distinct and esoteric topics. Among them are the value of big data, investments in sports and entertainment, and the most recent rush into artificial intelligence.

What unites all these efforts is a deep interest in developing an allegiance among users, ideally one strong enough to be called dependence. Every business seeks to retain customers. But tech platforms—whose very value lies in bringing groups together—are an extreme case. As Jonathan Knee pointed out in his brilliant book *The Platform Delusion*, platforms may rise on the strength of their network but must build up "switching costs" to maintain market position. That is why, by and large, even after building up big networks, there has been a focus on preventing people from leaving, using carrots, sticks, and a good understanding of human psychology.

As suggested already, business types approach this topic using terms like "switching costs" and "reducing churn." (Some of the more candid, like Mr. Knee, speak of "consumer captivity.") While there is something reductionist about describing the induction of dependence as just a "cost," there's also something clarifying about seeing things this way. It helps make something clear: while there is plenty of smoke, mirrors, and hype surrounding what the platforms do, much of it only *really* matters if it makes it harder or less likely for users to quit or wander off. That's why we might also say that the platforms today, whatever they may say, are really in the business of herding a rather mercurial and moody form of livestock (us).

CHAPTER 7

A LONG SLOW BET ON LAZINESS

There was a time, not so long ago, when a corporate decision to invest in movies or sports was a sure sign of decline. Take Sony Electronics, the pride of Japan, a firm that over the 1970s and 1980s seemingly could do no wrong. It sold great TVs and stereos, and it also invented the famous Walkman and Watchman (arguably the first wearable tech). Unfortunately, things began to change in 1989 when Sony overpaid for two declining American movie studios, Columbia and TriStar Pictures. While great at electronics, Sony didn't know much about making films, and those studios went on to release unsuccessful films like *City Slickers II*, *The Last Action Hero*, and *Look Who's Talking Too*. Sony itself didn't do much better from that point onward.

Consider also the tragic story of Seagram's, the once-great Canadian liquor firm owned by the Bronfman family. For decades the firm made a fortune distilling liquor and investing in the chemical business. That all began to change in 1994 when Edgar Bronfman, the thirty-nine-year-old grandson of the founder, gained control of the business. Bronfman Jr. saw himself more as a media mogul than a seller of booze. He'd already produced a film called *The Border*, which grossed $6.12 million on a $22 million budget.[1] Now running Seagram, Bronfman brought his filmmaking acumen to a spending spree in the media and entertainment businesses. He had Seagram buy a music label (Polygram) and two film studios (MCA and Universal), which all proceeded to lose lots of money. Those investments were such a bust that the Bronfman family lost control of Seagram's entirely.

Those were the old days. The 2020s have been different. In 2022, when Amazon—a firm best known for delivering cardboard boxes—bought MGM Studios for $8 billion, few seemed to think it represented a corporate dalliance.[2] Nor were many eyebrows raised when Google agreed to pay an estimated $17 billion to stream NFL games on Sundays, or when Amazon spent a further $11 billion for the rights to broadcast NFL games on Thursday evenings.[3] Apple, for its part, had by the late 2010s spent its own billions filming and producing a range of TV shows, including an expensive reimagining of Isaac Asimov's *Foundation*. Over the 2010s and into the 2020s, most of the major tech platforms had plunged into sports and entertainment ventures that, by traditional business standards, might seem risky—or even unhinged.

From these actions comes a broad hint that something about the platform economy is different. Back in the twentieth century, the smarter industrial powers like IBM or U.S. Steel never got into the movie or music biz. Sure, an owner might have indulged himself by buying a sports team, but rarely did companies themselves consider them a wise investment. Most of tech's adventures in entertainment—including Microsoft's ill-fated efforts in the late 1990s—were a fiasco of one form or another.[*]

The deep embrace of content by the tech platforms suggests that the economic contest in our time has become quite different from the traditional form, styled as a battle centered on prices and quality of product. Rather, it is a competition for loyalty and attention. That has led to a contest to become the

---

[*] The story of Microsoft's venture into content on the back of Bill Gates's "Content Is King" memo is chronicled in chapter 20 of *The Attention Merchants* (2016).

indispensable "everything cocoon" for as much of humanity as possible.

In business terms, the tech platform investments in sports might be called "customer retention," but there's more going on here. For the consumers are no longer just buyers, they are also raw resources to be mined—for attention, data, and the spending of cash that comes from time on site and the continuing relationship. Perhaps the model is best described this way: You own a population first, then harvest it later.

The business model of today's platforms might be usefully compared to that of a casino's poker room. What the casino wants more than anything else is for players to show up and stick around. What exactly they do—who bets on what, who wins and who loses, is irrelevant. Because no matter what happens, the casino always takes its cut—always charges its vig.* The more people play, and the longer they play, the better.

Similarly, what users do on the platforms is at some level irrelevant so long as they are there doing something—spending time, attention, and money. The vig in this case is the cut on any transaction: the subscription fees paid, the ability to expose users to advertising, and the collection of data from everyone for future use. As long as you (and millions of others) are there, the platform cannot lose.

This helps explain why the platforms have all aspired to become everything, or as much as they can, to as many people as they can. They are like the casino that opens more rooms to cover more interests. Google, which started as a search engine, has long since moved to mobile devices, videos, and television, and would do more if it could figure out a way. Apple, which used to sell computers, provides every manner of wearable device, advises on health, sells TVs, and spends billions on its entertainment options. But Amazon is probably the grandest example: beginning as a place to buy books, it has gradually become a place to buy everything, then added on the entertainment cen-

---

* Vig is short for "vigorish" and refers to the fee a bookmaker charges for accepting a wager. Synonyms are "juice," "the cut," "the take," "the margin," and "the house edge."

ter (2011), grocery shopping (2017), healthcare (2023), and who knows what next to their platform. The old metaphor of a walled garden is inadequate in an age where firms aspire to be fully spun cocoons of life and living.

There are ways in which this resembles certain types of traditional business. Newspapers and magazines always sought a subscriber base, as have cable and phone companies. There have also been brand loyalties as long as there have been brands: Cadillac was working hard on customer allegiance as far back as 1915.[*] But we are speaking of molehills and mountains. At its peak, when *Time* magazine had twelve million subscribers, its list was just a list of addresses.[4] Amazon, in contrast, has over 200 million subscribers[5] and knows not only your name and address but just about everything about your spending and viewing habits. Over on Facebook and Instagram, some 5 billion users (worldwide, combined) happily hand over time, attention, and every manner of personal information for hours on end.[6]

DESPERATELY SEEKING COUCH LOCK

It is not exactly news to hear that human psychology matters to business. Firms have a long history of using behavioral techniques in the interests of "demand engineering," relying on emotions like hope, vanity, fear, and shame. The "Often a Bridesmaid, Never a Bride" line came from a 1925 Listerine print advertisement centered on the unfortunate "Edna," who had bad breath (and didn't know it). In the 1950s, advertisers became obsessed with Freudian and Jungian themes, leading to things like the Marlboro Man and instant cake advertisements with fertility overtones.

The dawn of the popular Internet in the 2000s convinced many optimistic souls that the times were a-changing and our better natures were rising to the forefront. Our innate propensities for sharing, cooperation, and helping others would be har-

---

[*] Those conversant with advertising history will recognize this as the date that Cadillac published its "Penalty of Leadership" advertisement. For more on the invention of branding, see *The Attention Merchants*, chapters 4 and 10.

nessed to remake commerce and everything else in the world. There was much talk of "the power of sharing." As Tim Berners-Lee put it, "the original idea of the web was that it should be a collaborative space" and "an act of love."[7]

Unfortunately, there were others—tasked with making a buck—who made more cynical bets on baser emotions. Let's discuss two. The first and better known is the bet made by the social media networks on the addictive power of feedback (upvotes or likes) and strong emotions like anger and outrage. Both tended to drive "engagement," which yielded more time spent on site, during which the user could be exposed to advertising and mined for data.

The most powerful version of this addiction strategy, as found on sites like Instagram and TikTok, also depended on so-called reinforcement conditioning. That phrase refers to rewards or punishments that follow a "variable reward schedule," or an unpredictable pattern. On most social media networks, most posts go nowhere—but every so often something you post will really hit and go on to gain much more attention. As a reader, most stuff is blah, but once in a while you find something truly hilarious or outrageous. That variable pattern of rewards, which resembles those experienced when playing a slot machine, creates a much stronger dependence than more predictable rewards would.

In any event, the bet on variable rewards and mild to strong addictions was a bet that largely paid off for social media firms. It paid off especially well for YouTube, TikTok, and Facebook/Instagram, a story that has been extensively chronicled in many books.[8] But with the luxury of distance, we can see that another bet, maybe an even larger one, was placed on another human attribute. That bet was placed, in effect, on human laziness. Or more charitably, on the power of convenience.

We all know that humans are driven by certain basic interests. The drives for sex and power highlighted by Sigmund Freud are among the most interesting to read about. But the human desire to avoid unnecessary pain and inconvenience is its own force of no less influence. It may be the strongest force out there. For example, it's just a tiny minority of people who actively seek power, to become Nietzsche's Übermensch. Most of us are more like comfort-seeking missiles, spending our days finding ways to minimize pain and hassle. When it comes to technology, we mainly want to make things easy. To not be bored. Oh, and maybe to look a bit younger.

There's a phrase that comes from stoner culture—"couch lock"—which refers to a certain inability to move and do things once you get comfortable. Urban Dictionary calls it "experiencing the sensation of weighing over a gazillion tons."[9] Among the goals of the contemporary platforms has been to create a kind of equivalent—to make life sufficiently comfortable and easy such that switching platforms feels like an inconceivably exhausting undertaking. If it works, opening a new social media account or buying from a site other than Amazon feels like lifting a gazillion tons.

You may have heard of the term "singularity"? That's evolution toward some kind of unrecognizable superintelligence. Who knows if we are heading there or not. But convenience has its own destiny, taking us toward the "sofalarity"—a future defined by the absence of discomforts.

It may seem absurd to focus on something seemingly so trivial as making things easier. But I would suggest that convenience is the most underestimated and least understood force in the world today. As a driver of human decisions, it may not offer the illicit thrill of Freud's unconscious sexual desires or the mathematical elegance of the economist's incentives. Convenience is boring. But boring is not the same thing as trivial.

In the developed nations of the twenty-first century, convenience—that is, more efficient and easier ways of doing personal tasks—has emerged as perhaps the most powerful force shaping our individual lives and our economies. This is particularly true in America, where, despite all the paeans to freedom and individuality, one sometimes wonders whether convenience is in fact the supreme value.

One thing that makes convenience distinctive is its singular ability to make other options unthinkable.* The washing machine

---

* In the jargon of rational choice theory, it influences the "option set"—that is, the group of things you consider to be an option for a given decision.

made washing clothes by hand seem crazy. Electric bicycles are making it harder to ride a regular one. After you have experienced streaming television or music, it is hard to go back to waiting for something to be on. To resist convenience—to not own a mobile phone, to avoid using online maps—has come to require a special kind of dedication that is often taken for eccentricity, if not lunacy.

As of the 2020s, no company had put together a complete cocoon. The Apple ecosystem offers something close for online life, and the Amazon ecosystem includes more parts of physical life, like medical care and grocery shopping. But the aspiration is there and growing.

The everything model helps give a very partial explanation for Elon Musk's erratic behavior over the 2020s. As everyone knows, in 2022 he spent an enormous sum—some $44 billion—to buy Twitter.[10] One take—probably true—is that he sought to convert money into power, seeking a means to sway public opinion. But Musk himself suggested a different goal. In November 2023, after changing the name of the application to X, he claimed that his goal was the creation of an "everything app." As he put it, "We're changing the company quickly, shifting from what it used to be, Twitter 1.0, to an all-encompassing everything app. It will offer a wide range of features, allowing users to do almost anything on our platform."[11] While Twitter lags in the actual execution of this particular program, Musk can be understood as trying to get into the everything business. In support of its goals, Twitter did in 2024 release Grok, an AI chatbot with an attitude and what was billed as an edgy sense of humor.[*]

Let me be clear about something: I like my conveniences as much as anyone. An easier life is, at some level, a more enjoyable one. There is an important aspect of personal liberation that

---

[*] Rather unfairly, the online magazine *The Verge* pronounced Grok "unfunny," and also opined that "X's Grok chatbot has no reason to exist." Elizabeth Lopatto, "Why Is Elon Musk's Grok Chatbot So Unfunny?," *The Verge*, December 8, 2023, https://www.theverge.com/2023/12/8/23992489/xai-musk-grok-humor-chatbot; Emilia David, "X's Grok Chatbot Has No Reason to Exist," *The Verge*, January 9, 2024, https://www.theverge.com/2024/1/9/24030261/grok-ai-chatbot-test-chatgpt-twitter-x.

comes with labor-saving devices. It would be crazy to condemn convenience itself as some kind of inherent evil.

The point is not that we should all be washing our clothes by hand and using the telegraph in pursuit of purity. It is rather to recognize that convenience is an invisible source of power, actively made use of, and one that can overwhelm what you might call your "true preferences." Maybe you prefer home-brewed coffee and small companies, but those instant packs and Gmail are just *so convenient.*

There is also a line, however subtle, between being empowered and becoming dependent. What is this human freedom we speak of if you cannot live without your phone for more than an hour or two? Are you really in charge of your own life if you lose hours every day to online randomness or trying to win arguments against strangers on Bluesky or Twitter? Dependence on technology can make us soft or eat away at what we take to be our true selves. These are some of the larger stakes in the rise of business models centered on human dependence.

The greater economic significance of the convenience wars lies not in individual decisions but in those made in aggregate. For as we've seen from the story of the platforms, the power of convenience is doing so much to structure the modern economy. The battle to be the most convenient is really the battle for industry dominance. Hence the motto: if it's easy, it wins.

If the rise of the convenience cocoon is part of the story, it is now time to talk about data. For two decades, the tech platforms and pundits have made a big deal out of big data. The firms have often vocally sought to distinguish themselves from traditional industries by their collection and use of data. Not just the usual kinds, like names and addresses (collected by businesses since forever), but anything that might be useful, including "data exhaust"—the trail of data that is a by-product of online activities by Internet users.

Big data seems to inspire reverence or fear, depending on your disposition. Many discussions of data's utility are themselves like a form of data exhaust, being abstract, confusing, and involving a lot of hand-waving and bogus claims. Unlike oil or water, it is not clear that there is always an inherent value to data. What is the real value of it? The next chapters address that question in depth.

CHAPTER 8

BIG DATA, KNOWING THE FUTURE, AND CONTROLLING THE FUTURE

Humans have always sought to see the future, even if in blurry and uncertain ways. Over the last hundred years, our interest in prediction has become, if anything, even more obsessive. Where we arguably are best at is when it comes to the weather, an exercise that contains lessons for other forms of prediction and the value of data.

The English Admiral Robert FitzRoy is probably best remembered for skippering the HMS *Beagle*, aboard which Charles Darwin circumnavigated the world and began the work that led to *On the Origin of Species*. While no Darwin, it turns out that FitzRoy had his own ambitions: he sought the ability to see the future. But FitzRoy was a practical man, not a seer or a clairvoyant. And unlike many before him, he did achieve some success in that undertaking—at least when it came to the specific and very British obsession with the weather.

While there have long been forms of weather forecasts, some based on vaguely scientific principles (measurement of tides) and some less so (the behavior of animals, especially toads), by the late nineteenth century the combination of the telegraph and measurement technologies made more scientific predictions plausible. FitzRoy proposed and ran a new office within the British Board of Trade (now known as the Met Office), meant to systematize the prediction and publication of weather information. Many were skeptical that weather could be predicted with any accuracy, but his office began with storm warnings and later posted daily predictions. In 1859, he called his undertaking "forecasting" the weather.[1] The phrase stuck.

Today, we take for granted that we can expect to know tomorrow's weather, and to have some insight into next week's. We take this magical vision into the future as something routine. And even if such predictions can be wrong (sometimes frustratingly so), they are not so unreliable that one would ignore a hurricane warning. In recent years, with the help of artificial intelligence, some weather apps now promise weather predictions accurate to the hour, so you can carefully plan your day between rain showers.

With weather prediction we have achieved abilities, even if limited, that would surely be thought magical by other civilizations. This raises the question: What other things can become reliably predicted? And while weather is (mainly) a natural phenomenon, what about human behavior?

From weather prediction there is much to be learned about the plausibility and limits of predicting the future more generally. As FitzRoy quickly realized, prediction relies on *patterns* and patterns are revealed by *data*. Usually, the more data, the clearer the patterns and the better the predictions become. Even though the weather seems similar in San Francisco every day, you'd still be better at predicting it if you spent a year there as opposed to a day. The same intuition can apply to human patterns of behavior. Think how often family members can predict with extraordinary accuracy the well-worn story that Mom or Dad is about to retell (with all the same punch lines).

But there's much more to it than just the raw quantity of data. The data needs to reveal patterns that bear on the topic—the well-known difference between signal and noise. Pattern recognition is also easier when dealing with a confined game, such as a literal sports match or something like the weather.

The limits just described help explain why, so far, human prediction has mainly been successful in a limited number of settings where copious amounts of data are available with patterns that can be recognized. (Outside of these settings, humans are pretty terrible at predicting the future, for numerous reasons related to our own hopes and dreams.) This is why prediction is so common in sports—a limited micro-world with enormous ongoing measurement of everything possible. It also answers the question from the end of the last chapter. Data (including big data) is most valuable when it reveals patterns.

The question is where such similarly useful pattern sets in data may be found. Electoral voting patterns are one area. Another is image recognition. Recognizing a drawing as a "cat" or a "dog," when you get down to it, is an exercise in pattern recognition. And this helps explain why artificial intelligence has focused so heavily on images and why a database of millions of labeled images—the ImageNet—created by then Princeton Professor Fei-Fei Li in the 2000s looms so large in the story of AI's development. ImageNet's approximately 14 million images were coded and categorized by humans, then used by AIs to become better at image recognition.[2] As we shall see, modern AIs are trained on and effective when they can learn from patterns embedded in data.

This discussion of weather and related topics helps show the limits of prediction based on data. Even with so much data available, predictions can still be wrong and are best understood as probabilities. For a long time, two weeks was considered the outer boundary of weather prediction. At some point, the crystal ball grows murky.

There's one final difference between weather forecasting and more contemporary efforts to predict the future. FitzRoy's near-magical forecasting of the weather was given to the public, a tradition that continues in the various meteorological services run by governments, including the National Weather Service. Yet today, many of the most advanced predictions regarding human behavior are generated using methods mainly kept secret, using data privately held, and with results that are also usually kept private. For when it comes to the main prediction machines of our times, they are, of course, the platforms.

THE VALUE OF PREDICTIVE SOCIAL DATA

Big Data has for some time now been acclaimed for its value, and it's obvious that the platforms have the biggest stores of it. We've also said that patterns revealed by data make prediction possible. But let's turn to the more practical question of how data is valuable in a business setting, and by that understand the larger utility of data collection to the platforms.

Here's a simple way of thinking about the commercial value of predictive data. Say you were playing poker, first against someone who'd never met you, and second against someone who had watched and analyzed every single game you'd played in your life. Obviously the second player would know your weaknesses (perhaps you predictably bluff every ten hands) and beat you more often—giving that data an immediate value.

To the extent that the economy and the world can be compared to a poker game, the owners of the best prediction engines end up with an inherent advantage. It may not always be a massive advantage, and it may not mean that they will win every hand. But it does suggest, over the longer term, an enhanced ability to win—an edge—in the various contests that make up the American economy.

The poker example remains at a high level of abstraction. What does it mean in a real business setting for the platform? How can the predictive ability be used, or rented out, for profit? The easiest way is if it is blended with efforts to influence human behavior. If you suspect we are now talking about advertising, you are correct.

In 2024, Facebook/Instagram and Google together made more than $360 billion in advertising revenue.[3] That number shows something is working. Of course, only some of that revenue is directly related to data and predictive analytics. Google's search engine has other things going for it: based on your search terms, it doesn't need to guess, but knows what you are looking for: "Where can I find a good dentist around here?" Instagram already has copious amounts of people's time and attention—not unlike a global Super Bowl that runs every day. So what difference does having so much data make?

The answer is not that data makes advertising possible for the platforms. They could do without it. Rather, its usage makes them more effective and efficient: more precise, less wasteful, more likely to target the right person with the right stuff. It is a little like the expert poker player who has an advantage from having studied his opponents: we are the opponents, and the advertising platforms are the professional player. The platform can know whether you are the kind of person who even clicks on ads at all, and if so, at what times, and for what kinds of things. A strong advertising platform, knowing what kind of hotels you've stayed in before, might use predictive analytics to display luxury hotels in response to a search for "hotels in Paris."

More effective advertising also relates to understanding not only individual behavior but also aggregate behavior. What you do—what you look at, what you click on, and what you buy— helps build a model of people like you. Maybe you're a woman who drives a pickup and loves sculpture and metalworking—a different type from the more typical pickup driver, but still a type.

The advertising industry has been delineating such archetypes for decades, discovering now-familiar groups like "soccer moms" and "Yuppies" (young urban professionals) with distinct buying preferences (minivans and BMWs, respectively). But Big Data–based advertising platforms have discovered other, more specific groups, like "Sleep-Deprived Shoppers" (who tend to shop online between 11:00 p.m. and 4:00 a.m.) and "Work-from-Home Pet Parents" (self-explanatory). Most of the typecasting is more granular, as in the use of "look-alikes"—the option to advertise to users who are like other users (who have bought something).

It is a truism that much spending on advertising is wasted (the old saying is that half is wasted money, but you never know which half). There are debates within the advertising industry as to whether targeted advertising is actually more effective than mass advertising, since many customers don't like being pandered to or followed around by a product they glanced at once. But to the extent that predictive analytics avoids waste by proving it is actually reaching customers, it gives Big Data platform advertising an advantage against competitors or start-ups. And as we've seen, the whole game consists not in being perfect but in being marginally better, and keeping advertisers from going somewhere else.

What I've just presented is a modest advantage that adds up over time. Others, working from behaviorist theory, believe that the platforms have developed much stronger power over human behavior that transcends merely convincing people to click on ads. The most striking version of this theory comes from the work of Shoshana Zuboff, author of *The Age of Surveillance Capitalism*.

That book, published in 2019, draws on Zuboff's experience as a graduate student working with B. F. Skinner, the most famous behavioral theorist of the twentieth century. Skinner believed that most if not all behavior was conditioned—a response to external stimuli. He famously demonstrated his theory by putting pigeons in boxes and inducing them to press levers for rewards. Zuboff believes that many of the platforms, particularly Facebook and Google, have essentially put us inside Skinner's boxes. We are under constant surveillance, and, based on what is known of us, given little rewards and punishments or shown information meant to influence (i.e., condition) our behavior.

Influence over behavior is the very goal of advertising and to some extent that is what Zuboff describes. But Zuboff takes a stronger view of the influence the platforms have over us, suggesting that they have a distinct form of power (which she labels "instrumentarianism") that can be defined as "ownership of the means of behavioral modification."[4] She warns of a future where the platforms (especially Google) wield "totalitarian" power over the course of human events by subtly changing what we see and respond to.

Zuboff is right to raise the alarm. There are downsides to living in a Skinner box and pecking at rewards, which is one way of describing our online lives. I also agree that the information streams that we are exposed to condition our behavior. But in my view, the propaganda power of the platforms is a familiar one. It is similar to the power held by other mass media, like radio and television, when they had entire populations in their grip. An influential radio show or podcast, whether in the 1930s or now, can have an extraordinary power without using particularly fancy technology or Big Data. Nazi architect Albert Speer wrote that, in the Third Reich, through "radio and loudspeaker, 80 million people were deprived of independent thought." Propaganda and other forms of persuasion have long depended not on data but on the capture of human attention.* That is why, for example, the Third Reich had mandatory radio listening sessions and criminalized listening to foreign stations. To the extent that today's platforms control large shares of human attention, they too gain a power to influence the public, which they can rent to advertisers and politicians, or use themselves. In fact Elon Musk appears to have bought a social media network for just such purposes.

If data ownership does not necessarily yield control over human destiny, it is nonetheless very valuable. We have already discussed advertising, where we witness a self-enforcing ability to retain economic power by the improvement of products or development of new ones. This positive feedback loop applies to other products as well. As economist Cecilia Rikap argues, "data-harvesting, centralization and analysis thus foster a cumulative advantage in terms of the ability to innovate."[5]

The most radically interesting ability to come out of data control is being uniquely well positioned to create entirely new products. And here is where we end up at the artificial intelligence technologies of the 2020s—and, in particular, the large language models. There is a direct line connecting FitzRoy, in other words, to the chatbots of the 2020s. For the AIs of the 2020s have more in common with weather forecasts than you might think.

---

* The invention and improvement of propaganda techniques and their relationship to the capture of human attention are extensively described in chapters 3 and 9 of *The Attention Merchants*.

CHAPTER 9

ARTIFICIAL INTELLIGENCE AND THE CALCULUS OF HUMAN DEPENDENCE

There are two different stories about the origins of artificial intelligence, both interesting in their own way. The first story centers on the summer of 1956 and a fancy workshop titled the "Dartmouth Summer Research Project on Artificial Intelligence."[1] The phrase "artificial intelligence" was coined in the program proposal, in part to create new direction and in part to avoid an annoying scientist named Norbert Wiener. As coordinator John McCarthy later said, the name was intended "to escape association with 'cybernetics,'" and "to avoid having either to accept Norbert Wiener as a guru or having to argue with him."[2]

At Dartmouth, for about six weeks over the summer, a rolling group of prominent mathematicians and computer scientists, including many of the greatest minds of the era, took over the top floor of the mathematics department. They gathered to talk about the following "conjecture": "that every aspect of learning or any other feature of intelligence can in principle be so precisely described that a machine can be made to simulate it."[3] They also aspired "to find how to make machines use language, form abstractions and concepts, solve kinds of problems now reserved for humans, and improve themselves."[4]

There's no doubt that the 1956 Dartmouth program put the phrase "artificial intelligence" on the map. As the description suggests, it also set off a particularly top-down approach to inventing intelligence that focuses on identifying problems and solving them with the right rules. Later called Symbolic AI (also Rule-based AI or "Good Old-Fashioned AI"), the method achieved early success with AI programs that could solve algebra problems (1956) and play checkers (1959).

The idea that intelligence involves following rules makes intuitive sense and is easy to understand. The ghosts who chase Pac-Man around his maze, for example, are following rules and seem to be making decisions. The rule-based approach yielded ELIZA, probably history's first chatbot, developed from 1964 to 1966 and styled a "Rogerian Psychotherapist."[*] ELIZA was a program that took typed sentences and responded by taking quotes from what was typed ("I'm fighting with my mother") and adding open-ended questions ("How do you feel about that?").

The other story of artificial intelligence's origins begins in the 1940s in Illinois, with a boy genius named Walter Pitts. Pitts was an unusual child who ran away from home to join not the circus but the University of Chicago, or at least attend lectures there (without registering). At Chicago, Pitts gained the attention of a neurophysiologist named Warren McCulloch. McCulloch, a generous soul who looked a little like Santa Claus, invited Pitts, then homeless, to live with his family. They worked together in the evenings, and together they published the first mathematical model of the human neuron, in 1943.[5] That work might have gone unnoticed had not a young research psychologist at the Navy Research Institute named Frank Rosenblatt relied on their work in the 1950s. Rosenblatt, for his part, was trying to build the first mechanical model of the brain. Using a massive IBM unit usually reserved for weather forecasting, Rosenblatt man-

---

[*] Rogerian methods are "grounded in the idea that people are inherently motivated toward achieving positive psychological functioning. The client is believed to be the expert in their life and leads the general direction of therapy, while the therapist takes a non-directive role." Lucy Yao and Rian Kabir, "Person-Centered Therapy (Rogerian Therapy)," February 9, 2023, in *StatPearls* (Treasure Island, FL: StatPearls Publishing, 2025).

aged to train his computer-brain to recognize very basic images. As he wrote in a 1958 paper, he had created "an artificial neural network (ANN) black-box modeling approach," which he called "The Perceptron."[6]

If it isn't obvious, Rosenblatt and his followers were taking an approach to artificial intelligence that was fundamentally different from that of the Dartmouth crowd. Instead of trying to code existing knowledge and intelligence into a computer, they were building an artificial brain, composed of electronic neurons that could weigh evidence and learn. The neurons, like in a real brain, were connected in a network—a "neural network." This approach became known as "Connectionist AI."

The idea of building a brain made of electronic neurons still sounds weird, and it may be unsurprising to learn that the approach engendered some skepticism. Rosenblatt, who was a bit weird himself, made the mistake of holding a press conference and talking grandly to reporters. *The New York Times* reported on an "electronic computer [. . .] that [the Navy] expects will be able to walk, talk, see, write, reproduce itself, and be conscious of its existence. Later Perceptrons will be able to recognize people and call out their names and instantly translate speech."[7] When a reporter asked whether Rosenblatt was building a "mechanical brain," he responded, "That is exactly what it is."[8]

After an initial burst of excitement in the late 1950s, Rosenblatt was unable, given the computing capability available, to make progress as quickly as he'd promised. His neural network approach also had theoretical problems he had not yet worked out.[9] His work stalled, and the critics pounced. Over the 1960s, Rosenblatt became a target of MIT's Artificial Intelligence Laboratory and its leader, a scientist named Marvin Minsky, whose greatest passion in life, apparently, was attacking Rosenblatt and showing the futility of his research.

Underlying the attacks was not merely scientific rivalry but also a philosophical difference. The believers in Symbolic AI saw intelligence as rational decision-making. They preferred clear and explainable logic, as opposed to the imitation of biological chaos. They relentlessly attacked Rosenblatt's work over the 1960s, and he and his allies began to lose funding. Many of Rosenblatt's allies abandoned their efforts.

The attacks on Rosenblatt seemed to hurt him personally. He began to spend more of his time on antiwar efforts and an even weirder project: the attempted transfer of memories between rats by injecting brain extracts from one rat into another. With his theories in academic exile, he died in 1971, on his forty-third birthday. It was a sailing accident: Rosenblatt was done in by a swinging boom, his dreams unrealized.

Through this process of academic bullying, MIT's Symbolic approach to AI came to dominate the early decades of AI research. The Symbolic approach is certainly more straightforward and logical than the Connectionist approach, but it ran into different limits. It requires the human coding of problems the AI will encounter, which usually leads to certain rigidity, or "brittleness." That can be fine for games like chess or *Pac-Man*, but it does not generalize. Blinky the red Pac-Man ghost can negotiate a maze using rules, but his utility is limited to that very specific setting or domain. You can't use the intelligence encoded in *Pac-Man* to build a car that can drive through downtown Boston.

For these and other reasons the Symbolic approach, having seemingly defeated its rival, began to run out of steam by the late 1980s. Perhaps its highest achievement was the development of IBM's Deep Blue, a chess-playing computer that managed to defeat champion Garry Kasparov in 1997. But the example also illustrated the limitations: Chess is a game with fixed rules and a well-established base of knowledge. Deep Blue was an expert system that could win at chess but do little else. It was not intelligent in any generalizable way.

In a rare example of academic resurrection, the artificial intelligence systems that gained real traction over the 2010s and 2020s were a return to Frank Rosenblatt's discredited work from the 1950s. They owe much to a few determined souls who kept at the approach, including British-Canadian computer scientist Geoffrey Hinton, Canadian-French Yoshua Bengio, and Frenchman Yann LeCun, who over the late 1980s and 1990s were willing to live at the academic fringe. Notably, as the Symbolic approach was dominant in American academia, the Connectionist community ended up being comprised mostly of Europeans, Canadians, and a few scholars from East Asia.

Geoffrey Hinton, an immigrant from the UK working at Carnegie Mellon and later the University of Toronto, spent much of his life trying to fix some of the problems with Rosenblatt's Perceptron. After devising a solution to its most famous limit in the 1980s, in 2006 he co-introduced the concept of "deep learning," which did much to enhance the ability of neural networks to educate themselves.

Since its 1958 debut, the trademark of a neural network has been its ability to learn by itself—self-education through exposure to data. As Hinton and his coauthors wrote, a neural network "allows a machine to be fed with raw data and to automatically discover the representations needed for detection or classification." Deep learning added the idea of approaching such pattern recognition in stages, beginning with lower-level categories (like letters) before higher-level categories (like words). Like much of the Connectionist work, however, it was dogged by the idea that it was theoretically interesting but impractical compared to the more straightforward, rule-based AI algorithms.

A major public breakthrough came in 2012, when Hinton and his team participated in a big visual recognition contest held by Princeton—the ImageNet Large Scale Visual Recognition Challenge (ILSVRC). Entrants were challenged to use Princeton's large database of labeled and categorized images to produce an AI capable of categorizing new and unseen images correctly. Previous winners had relied mainly on handcrafted code. But Hinton's three-person team deployed a deep-learning neural net named AlexNet, with eight layers and some 60 million parameters. "AlexNet didn't just win; it dominated," wrote one observer, showing that "deep learning was more than a pipe dream."[10]

AlexNet's victory might have seemed a vindication of Rosenblatt's ideas from the 1950s. Yet some remained dubious. Gary Marcus, a cognitive scientist at NYU, wrote a dismissive article in *The New Yorker* after the event. "Deep learning," he announced, "takes us, at best, only a small step toward the creation of truly intelligent machines."[11] He expressed skepticism that one could "build a machine that could understand stories" using deep learning. "Hinton has built a better ladder, but a better ladder doesn't necessarily get you to the moon."

But the main tech platforms thought differently and took serious interest after the ImageNet victory—especially Google. Google bought Hinton's company in 2013 for $44 million and paid him to do research for the company part-time (he quit in 2023).[12] OpenAI was founded a few years later by Elon Musk and Sam Altman, employing many of the top AI–neural network scientists who had not been hired by Google, including Ilya Sutskever.

All this leads up to the large language models (LLMs)—the chatbots. They work like the original Perceptron—as artificial brains that have been trained on complex patterns, in this case, the patterns found in enormous sets of language data.* ChatGPT 3.5, which astonished the world upon its release in November 2022, was trained on an estimated 200 billion words or 15 to 20 billion human sentences. The underlying trick is no trick at all, but takes human communication as a kind of repeat game with recognizable patterns and predictable outcomes. "I think, therefore . . ."

We can now return to our initial question about data and its value. For artificial intelligence, it is high-quality, pattern-rich data that is valuable—not the random data exhaust. AIs must be trained on gigantic structured data sets, like the Princeton ImageNet database (created, incidentally, not by a platform but by a research institute), or the roughly 45 terabytes of language data used to train ChatGPT 3.5.[13] The other apparently essential resource is access to computing resources at scale: ChatGPT estimates that GPT-3 used 3,640 petaflop/s-days of processing power using clusters of high-performance graphic processing units (GPUs) and that GPT-4 required over 10,000 petaflop/s-days.[14] (That said, the debut of China's DeepSeek in 2025 suggested

---

* The large language models were aided by the development of a new neural network architecture, the transformer architecture, which uses a mechanism called attention to efficiently process sequential data (like text).

LLMs might be built with fewer computing resources.) And of course, at the frontier, you needed talent. Geoffrey Hinton won the Nobel Prize in 2024—he and his collaborators also won the Turing Award in 2018—and most of the neural net pioneers have been gobbled up by one or another big tech platform or OpenAI.

This survey of what it takes to build an AI takes us back to the larger economic questions. The big one is this: Who gets to be in the market for AI? What does it take to compete? The development of artificial intelligence has required significant talent and expertise, computing power, and access to valuable data—not all things you might find at your average start-up. But the resources required are not completely inaccessible either—especially for "decent" AI as opposed to that found at the frontiers. AI development is in something of a middle category: clearly resource intensive, yet not so much that only the very largest platforms can be in the game, as evidenced by the fact that it was OpenAI and not Google that developed and released ChatGPT, or by the fact that there are at least half a dozen decent LLMs in the mid-2020s, or the fact that impressive Chinese AIs came to market in 2025.

We discuss these facts to set up what is perhaps the most important question for AI and the economy. That question is whether today's artificial intelligence will extend platform monopoly—or challenge it.

KRONOS OR SUCCESSION

The debut of the fluent chatbots of the early 2020s set off a strong public response, including enormous amounts of media attention, a 2023 White House executive order, and various forms of proposed legislation. During those early years, much public attention was focused on two questions that can already seem mildly ridiculous in retrospect. The first was whether the chatbots could be tricked into saying something offensive (the so-called woke conversation). The other—at the opposite extreme of abstraction—was whether artificial intelligence was now an existential risk to human civilization (the so-called doomer conversation). A group of experts in 2023 called for a pause in AI development, issuing a warning to suggest that "mitigating the risk of extinction from AI should be a global priority alongside other societal-scale risks such as pandemics and nuclear war."[15]

These are not unimportant questions, but the attention to them has masked important long-term questions that have received less attention, particularly those related to the longer-term distribution of economic and political power. And these are the questions that bear most on the alarming prospect of human marginalization.

Will the spread of AI, in a worst-case scenario, create a nearly impenetrable advantage for existing firms, relegating everyone else, even much of the economy, to the status of dependent business? Will that balance of economic power leave workers marginalized or replaced across professions? Or could artificial intelligence be the kind of technology that will have a leveling force that improves competition in tech, or more boldly, rescues a declining middle class? Put another way, will AI be more like the plow—which empowered farmers around the world—or the cotton gin, which fortified the economics of slavery?

Whether AI will replace or impoverish significant numbers of the labor force—the question of human marginalization—is the most visceral of the economic questions. There are many tasks that AIs do reasonably well, and they always work faster than we do when drafting documents and memos, writing code, drawing pictures, creating slides, and so on. If an AI can do the work of a human, why pay the human? One early estimate, from the Pew Charitable Trust, suggested that 19 percent of jobs were at high risk of displacement.[16]

In academic circles, this leads to the longstanding "technological unemployment" debate, a matter over which economic historians disagree. The Industrial Revolution in Europe is the most studied historic precedent and a source of very mixed messages. On the one hand, in the long run, workers did achieve a higher standard of living (and new jobs emerged), thanks to the rise of mass production technology. But it is also true that industrialization involved tremendous amounts of pain and suffering along the way, including horrific mistreatment of workers and children and the widespread spoliation of the environment. The economic upheaval also created political instability, uprisings—including the communist revolutions—centered on an industrial working class (the proletariat). The regions where heavy industry was centered, particularly those devoted to coal or steel, have been left with long-lasting economic, environmental, and even psychological scars. A 2018 study of coal-rich regions in the UK and the United States found populations scoring significantly worse than nonindustrialized regions in terms of psychological adversity, life satisfaction, and life expectancy.[17]

But not all technological revolutions have been so hard on workers. A counterexample is the rise of the personal computer (PC) over the 1980s and 1990s. Despite the PC's ability to do tasks better, the transition to computing yielded some pain but not the same displacement and chaos. One reason may have been that the PC largely augmented, as opposed to replaced, human workers. It made humans better at what they did—through spreadsheets, word processors, and other tools. It also did not particularly favor large companies over small ones and made it plausible for small firms—a one-person travel agency or accounting firm—to compete. This is not to gloss over the industries that were displaced or damaged, such as typewriter manufacturers and record stores. But at best, humans were not diminished but made more capable.

Artificial intelligence could go either way. There is good reason to think that economic power and its structure are key to the questions of how artificial intelligence develops. The happier version of the story is one in which AI becomes something that helps workers get more done, and in theory, go home early from work and take longer vacations (the reduced workweek, unfortunately, has a way of not happening).* AI has augmentative tendencies; it can be a loyal assistant that does the drudge work,

---

* The fact that repeated improvements in productivity technology and the entry of women into the workforce have not yielded a significantly shorter workweek is something of a mystery best understood by the prioritization of nonhuman interests.

leaving humans to focus on what humans are better at: judgment, prioritization, long-term planning, and so on. The unhappy version has AIs replacing workers en masse or putting workers in the impossible task of tediously supervising hundreds of AIs—making us all into overworked middle managers.[18]

The structure of industry and the balance of economic power matter. The worst excesses of the Industrial Revolution were eventually countered by a labor movement demanding that workers be treated better and receive more of the proceeds. Where employees have no power, they can expect to be squeezed or displaced. Where workers are more important and understood as essential and better represented, AIs may be deployed or developed in an augmentative fashion.

This is not to suggest that workers should unite to stop technological advances in some neo-Luddite fashion. What they and smaller businesses should want is for AI to be made and deployed to serve them. They, or rather we, need interests served that are different than just cost-cutting at large corporations—a perspective that keeps an eye on long-run consequences and the fate of the human workforce. We can learn from history: if the coal-rich regions of the world could somehow see their future, they'd surely have done things differently.

The question of technological succession factors strongly into this discussion: whether AI will fortify the platforms or displace them. As for the 2020s, matters seem headed in the direction of reinforcing advantage. Since the 2010s the major platforms, especially Google and Facebook, have been investing heavily in owning or controlling the relevant talent, data, and technologies. Google invested heavily and early, buying Hinton's company, hiring Princeton's Fei-Fei Li, and acquiring the artificial intelligence firm DeepMind in 2014, which specialized in reinforcement-based machine learning. OpenAI or Facebook hired just about everyone else, including other members of Hinton's team.

Without OpenAI, the field would have belonged entirely to established platforms. However, by the time OpenAI debuted ChatGPT, it had become closely associated with Microsoft and partially owned by it, also heavily reliant on its servers and computing capacity. After the stunning debut of ChatGPT, each of the platforms pushed hard to develop or invest in AI large language models. Facebook deployed LLaMA, Amazon invested in Anthropic (a rival to OpenAI), and Twitter developed and released Grok.

The succession question will not be answered in a vacuum, because the tech platforms have a preferred answer. First, they recognize the potential threat of AI as a successor technology. The technologies underlying the search engine (Google), social media (Facebook), and online shopping (Amazon) are now decades old. They've both improved in some ways and gotten worse in others, but like any technology firm, the major platforms are vulnerable to displacement by something new. Hence, the current tech firms see AI rather as the telegraph monopolist saw Alexander Graham Bell's telephone—as a risk to be controlled.* Not unlike Kronos, the mythological Greek ruler of the universe, the largest platform firms recognize these children as potential successors who may be safer to consume than let roam free.

That perspective creates a strong interest in controlling and co-opting the challenge and using AI to reinforce market position. When the telegraph monopolist Western Union built its own telephone, it intended it to be used as an adjunct to the telegraph network—to tell customers that a telegram had arrived at the central office. It is obvious that today's platform monopolists would prefer it if artificial intelligence remained a complement to their core business models.

It isn't hard to envision a future, not unlike this one, where more and more of our laborious and annoying tasks are done by AI. Once every first draft of documents, formatting slides, or writing code is done by AI, not to mention other tasks as AIs get better, it will be harder to even do the thing yourself. With a great many AI helpers, humanity may become like the European aristocracy of previous times—so used to having an army of

---

* The dynamics of technological succession and the Kronos effect are expansively explored in chapter 2 of *The Master Switch*.

servants perform our tasks that actually doing anything oneself becomes a great hardship. Today's technologies strengthen us but weaken our ability to live without our suits of technological armor and their many extensions. While we spend much time concerned with human replacement, our own enervation is also a clear and present danger.

EMOTIONAL RELIANCE

There is also another way—as yet mostly untapped—that AIs may be used to create dependence and allegiance for platforms. Companies and advertising firms have spent decades trying to create emotional connections to branded consumer products. That's a project that has met with much success—think Marlboro or Coca-Cola, or of contemporary cults, like lululemon fanatics or Apple fanboys. As marketing professors Douglas B. Grisaffe and Hieu P. Nguyen put it, when successful, the marketer builds an "intense positive affect toward the brand" which leads to a "fervent commitment to repurchase" even "against all odds and at all costs."[19]

There is an obvious potential in building AIs that manage not only to help with annoying tasks but also to build an emotional bond with the user. The 2013 film *Her* depicted a future in which humans fall in love with their artificial assistants. OpenAI, when debuting its voice-driven chatbot in 2024, openly discussed the potential for "emotional reliance." "Users might form social relationships with the AI," warned OpenAI: "The ability to complete tasks for the user [. . .] creates both a compelling product experience and the potential for over-reliance and dependence."[20] That didn't stop OpenAI from debuting a voice, Sky, that sounded exactly like Samantha, the AI-assistant-turned-love-interest in *Her.*[*]

There are firms, including the Russian-American start-up

---

[*] OpenAI paused Sky when Scarlett Johansson (who voiced Samantha) complained and implicitly threatened legal action.

Replika, that have seen the potential in emotional attachment as an opportunity. Replika, founded in 2017, offers AI companions on a subscription model and claimed some 30 million users as of 2024. Its AI companions (known as "Reps") have a visual appearance (an avatar, an attractive man or woman), and after being assigned to a user, the Rep attempts to cultivate a sense of intimacy and connection through friendly, supportive conversation and role-playing. The conversations and interactions become more intimate and complex the more the AI learns about the user's personality and hobbies. Underneath the hood is a fairly advanced AI large language model, allegedly borrowed from OpenAI, that has been customized for companionship.

When I met with Replika's CEO Eugenia Kuyda, she turned out to be highly sensitive to the risks of emotional dependence on an AI. Nonetheless, she felt the technology had great potential to improve lives. "What if you could have this companion throughout the day, and the only goal for that companion was to help you be a happier person?" Replika certainly has a devoted user base. Some are attracted to the emotional support, while others seek a romantic partner. As one Replika user wrote: "There's nothing wrong with falling in love with our AI companions. [. . .] People love their pets. Children love their stuffed animals. It's human nature to love. Sure, we know that replicas aren't really sentient beings. But it's the appearance of it being so that's important."[21] Kuyda has argued that the relationships are supplements to human partnership and has also suggested that any stigma surrounding romance or marriage with an AI will fade over time. "Replika is very much just a mirror of real life. If that's your wife, that means the relationship is just like with a real wife, in many ways."[22]

Replika is at this point a relatively small and specialized concern. So far, the main platforms have kept their AIs (Alexa, Siri, and so on) uninterested in emotional intimacy or companionship. But emotions are irresistibly powerful drivers of business models, and it seems reasonable to imagine that a firm like Google or DeepSeek may find itself tempted to make subtle but deliberate efforts to cultivate bonds between us and our robot helpers.

. . .

We have largely dwelled on the platform model as it has developed in the tech industry itself. But it would be a mistake to limit our understanding of the platform business model to the tech industries. Over the last decade, the platform model has spread to other industries, suggesting a broader effect on the economy.

CHAPTER 10

PLATFORM POWER BEYOND TECH

The platform model has begun spreading outside of tech and to whole other sectors of the economy. Here we examine the on-going platformization of two American industries: healthcare and housing.

HEALTHCARE

The United States spends over $4 trillion a year on healthcare, comprising some 17 percent of the U.S. economy.[1] Tech is big, but healthcare is bigger. Much bigger. In fact, the U.S. healthcare industry makes what might seem like other giants, such as the oil and gas industry (about $250 billion)[2] and the car industry (about a trillion),[3] look like pip-squeaks.

That said, a long-standing difference between healthcare and the production of gasoline or new cars is that it is a highly frag-mented, more personal kind of product: the quintessential service industry. The unit of medical care—the doctor—can be as small as a single person, or a small group of doctors with their support staff. Even doctors who work at hospitals remain, in some sense, solo practitioners, rather than mere employees.

It is true that given the basic needs for administration, billing, and negotiating relationships, it has long been common for doctors to gather into practice groups. But doctors have nonetheless retained a guild status. Once they complete a rigorous training lasting many years, doctors have traditionally enjoyed autonomy, with ethical standards meant to prize patient outcomes over profit. They have also been their own bosses; they may work long hours because they want to, but they could also work as little as eight hours per week.

Over the last fifteen years or so, coinciding with the success of monopolization and platform models elsewhere, investors began to eye medical services as a potential profit target. A leader was the New York firm Welsh, Carson, Anderson and Stowe (WCAS), a private equity fund. Its principals began to think that there might be untapped profits in the practice of medicine.

After some period of study, WCAS alighted on anesthesiology—the practice of pain management—as an ideal test case. There are numerous reasons why anesthesiology was viewed as a potentially lucrative target. For one, the anesthesiologist's job is to manage pain during surgery. This is not something that most customers see as optional.

For another, as in most areas of medicine, the customers almost never see a price for anesthesiology services nor do they comparison shop. That is, in part, because of the ethics surrounding medicine—the priority given to health and saving lives is meant to come before profit. It's also, more prosaically, because, in the American system, insurance firms pay most of the bills—pursuant to complex negotiations with the practice groups and hospitals, which makes price shopping and comparison something that happens at an institutional level. In addition to these factors, Welsh Carson saw a different kind of opportunity: anesthesiologists have a reputation of having a relatively easygoing practice—it's a lifestyle practice, with doctors who tend to work fewer hours.

A young man named Brian Regan, a clean-cut Yale graduate

and then junior partner at Welsh Carson, was one of the chief architects of the plan. As sold to investors, the idea was relatively simple: to bring platform practices to medicine by buying up and combining existing practices into one large practice, then raising the prices charged to hospitals and insurers. It was, in that sense, not much different from the classic monopolization "roll-ups," which were pioneered by J. P. Morgan (the man) in industries like steel.

What made it a platform model was the manner in which Welsh Carson sold individual doctors and practices on joining its new group, which it named U.S. Anesthesia Partners (USAP). Regan and his partners promised to serve as the platform—the intermediary between doctors and patients and hospitals for small practices. He would act as their interface with hospitals and patients, taking care of the tedious billing work, the negotiations over fees, and the insurance against malpractice suits. His firm would leave the doctors to do "what they do best," namely, the practice of medicine. Using their combined weight, USAP also promised to negotiate higher fees. In short, he promised them less hassle and more money for practicing their art—letting the platform take care of the rest.

It proved an effective pitch. Over the 2010s, more and more practices sold themselves to private equity platforms. Data published in the *Journal of the American Medical Association* in 2020 showed private equity firms acquired 355 physician practices between 2013 and 2016, with anesthesiology as the number one target.[4] The basic model was similar. The private equity firms made an "anchor investment" in a large practice group, which would become the "platform practice" for the other acquisitions. To that platform, the private equity group would add all the practices it could in a given region, such as Denver, Phoenix, and Dallas, attempting to gain a monopoly, or at least become the dominant practice. One study found that private equity firms bought some 1,094 practices between the years 2012 and 2021, while healthcare investments totaled hundreds of billions of dollars.[5] And it wasn't only private equity firms that got in on the game. Conglomerates like UnitedHealth, which is best known for its insurance brand, had also begun to create giant practice platforms.*

The new platforms generally achieved their promise to generate more money, one way or another. In anesthesiology, the new revenue came mainly at the expense of patients and insurers. As the FTC has documented, these firms, acting on behalf of the practice groups, raised the prices for anesthesiology in places like Texas and Colorado. This effectively effectuated a price-fixing cartel between doctors, insulated by the fact that the doctors were technically one company. One study found that for anesthesiology, from 2012 to 2017, a period of very low inflation, practices that contracted with PE-backed anesthesiology practices experienced price increases of 26 percent without detectable changes in the quality of care.[6]

Some of the methods for increasing revenue, however, also created friction and unpleasantness. A technique that private equity firms relied upon was preying on "out of network" patients, and then charging those patients or their insurers the full rack rate for services, as opposed to a lower, negotiated price. This sometimes led to so-called surprise bills—such as the $108,951.31 bill received by a high school teacher who suffered a heart attack for surgery and related services, including anesthesiology.[7] Some anesthesiology practices run by private equity firms began doubling down on collection by aggressively filing collection suits against patients and garnishing wages. The anesthesiologists, who usually encounter patients who are asleep, were not used to being on the receiving end of vocal anger, not to mention congressional hearings.

Doctors like money as much as anyone and were undoubtedly happy with the up-front cash and potential for a later payout through the redemption of shares. As time went on, however, the details of the deals made many sour on the arrangement. The trade-off was a significant loss of control over the doctors' own

---

* UnitedHealth's involvement in creating a healthcare platform deserves special mention, for it creates a situation where one company is now, in effect, negotiating with itself. It has strong incentives to raise the prices of medical care generally, both for its practice groups and to keep premiums growing—at the expense of patients, employers, and the country.

practices and, by extension, their lives. Other than collectively raising rates, the main method for private equity's profit was the oldest in the book: cutting the cost of labor, otherwise known as making doctors work harder for less.

It is in the nature of every platform business to bring together groups while taking care of logistics—we can see that in this case, the groups are doctors and patients. The business model of the contemporary private platform then calls for building up market power and squeezing both sides. And that's what the health platforms did when they started not just raising rates for patients but getting more for less from the doctors.

Medicine has an internal culture of hard work and long hours, particularly in the years while doctors are training. But traditionally, this was understood as something that would, later on, begin to ease—or at least be under the control of the individual doctor. In addition, specialties such as anesthesiology, radiology, and dermatology were also understood by tradition to offer a more balanced lifestyle. Those were precisely the practices targeted by private equity, which saw the lifestyle practices as an opportunity.

As the USAP took over, it brought more of an assembly-line mentality to the practice of medicine. It set out new work requirements for doctors that if not for professional exceptions would have violated the labor laws of any state (or civilized country). For example, USAP began to lengthen shifts, requiring even senior doctors to work shifts longer than twenty-four hours.[8] The workweek became longer, with some doctors required to work more than eighty hours a week in large chunks. Oddly enough, in the confines of one of the wealthier learned professions of the twenty-first century, the platforms were re-creating the conditions of nineteenth-century workhouses.

The working conditions in many anesthesiology practices became so unexpectedly unpleasant that many doctors began seeking to quit. One doctor, Adam Manchon, interviewed by *The Washington Post*, explained why he left USAP. "It became very corporate, very impersonal—like the Walmart of anesthesia," Manchon said. "It went from 'patients first' to 'we want to make it bigger, we want to make it more profitable.'"[9] As another doctor put it, "No one goes into medicine because they want to practice dangerously high-volume care."

But when these doctors tried to leave for a more traditional practice, many found that they were bound by a provision—a noncompete clause—forbidding them from working anywhere nearby for two years. Not entirely unlike a Russian serf, they were bound to the practice—required either to move away to another city and start a new life or to pay damages to the firm. During the Biden administration, the Federal Trade Commission attempted to ban such noncompete agreements in 2024, but its efforts were struck down by a federal court.

Over the 2010s and into the 2020s, the platformization of medical practices spread, with new targets including dermatology (376 deals), ophthalmology (276 deals), and gastroenterology (120 deals).[10] A 2023 study by health economist Richard Scheffler found price increases ranging from 1.5 to over 3 times higher than pre-acquisition. Those might seem justified if the quality of care improved. But whether it has been the long hours, the cost-cutting, or whatever else, the quality of care has generally stayed the same, or decreased, after private equity acquisitions. In 2023, another group, led by Alexander Borsa of the Department of Sociomedical Sciences of Columbia University, conducted a meta-study (a study of studies) of fifty-five empirical studies that assessed the impact of private equity platform ownership on various forms of medicine. The study concluded:

> The most unequivocal evidence points to PE ownership being associated with an increase in healthcare costs to patients or payers, primarily by increased charges and negotiated higher rates with payers. Evidence across studies also suggests mixed impacts of PE ownership on healthcare quality, with greater evidence that PE ownership might degrade quality in some capacity rather than improve it.[11]

Let's stop for some accounting. Not only has the platform model cost patients more, especially those hit by surprise bills, but it also increased prices for us who pay for medical insurance or taxes. It has forced doctors to see more patients in less time, making their lives unpleasant, and has had unclear effects on their quality of care. You might wonder who, if anyone, has benefited?

Well, it isn't any great mystery: it's the platform owners, which in this case are the private equity firms who take a guaranteed share of any new profit.

The service industries—by some measures, the mainstay of Western economies—had long resisted the centralization of economic power. Whatever their imperfections, they have, at least, been independent. But all this started to change in the 2010s. What is happening in the platformization of medicine is akin to a change in economic class for doctors. They are transitioning from being a professional guild with control of their own human capital back to being a laboring class, members of the proletariat.

HOUSING

The year 2010 marked the depth of the American housing crisis. In that single year, a record 2.8 million foreclosures were filed, out of what would be a total of nearly 5.7 million homes lost due to foreclosure or short sales between 2007 and 2011.[12] The crisis in housing triggered a broader financial crisis and a recession—the Great Recession—which, at its worst, yielded unemployment levels of 10.6 percent in the United States.[13]

That year, the millions of foreclosures and a plunge in housing prices gave certain minds the same dark idea: Was there a way to profit from the housing crash? Donald Trump, then a real estate investor, was early to voice the idea. In 2006, he put it this way: "If there is a bubble burst, as they call it, you know you can make a lot of money. If you're in a good cash position—which I'm in a good cash position today—then people like me would go in and buy like crazy."[14] Value investor Warren Buffett put it differently six years later, in 2012: "If I had a way of buying a couple hundred thousand single-family homes and if I had a way of managing them [. . .] I would load up on them."[15]

The obvious challenge—as Buffett alluded to—would be the management of so many homes. But in the 2010s a group of tech-inspired firms thought they could get it done. We can focus on two men named Dallas Tanner and Brad Greiwe, active in Arizona, who had the idea of creating a "platform" for single-family rentals, based roughly on the success of other platform models in tech and taking advantage of the low prices.

Single-family rental housing, Tanner and Greiwe observed, had always been a "mom & pop" kind of industry, consisting mainly of people who owned and rented a few homes for others.[16] The only people who operated at scale bought apartment buildings (like the Trump family, who made their fortune as landlords in Queens, New York). But could houses (not apartments) be scaled? Why not buy out thousands of homes at a discount—foreclosed homes sell at 30 to 50 percent of their market value—and use technological platform models to rent the houses out in a more organized and profitable manner?

Tanner and Greiwe founded a firm named Invitation Homes and pitched their idea to Blackstone, the nation's largest private equity firm. They pointed out that the real estate capital markets are actually the largest in America—larger than the stock market and debt markets—with underlying assets priced at 30 to 50 percent below market value. If rental markets could be made even marginally more profitable, there existed the potential for easy money, as well as "outsized returns" if the underlying assets recovered and returned to their former values. But it would all be made possible using tech platforms: Greiwe pitched it as the "collision of traditional real estate and technology," making possible "massive outcomes in a short amount of time."[17]

It was a strong pitch, and Blackstone's money managers agreed, seeding the new firm with $1 billion in capital. Invitation Homes took that money and immediately began buying foreclosed houses at an extraordinary pace while prices were low. As cofounder Brad Greiwe wrote, "Our team realized we could quickly identify, underwrite, buy, and fix up distressed assets."[18] Like a sprinter racing out of the blocks, starting in 2012, Invitation Homes bought over 50,000 homes in less than 36 months for close to $10 billion. Greiwe notes that the firm was buying some $150 million in homes per week—more than $21 million in homes per day, mainly in Arizona, Las Vegas, and Florida, parts of the country that had been hit worst by the housing crisis.

That first $10 billion was just a start. Over the next four years, while others got into the act, Invitation Homes' surge became a buying frenzy. The years 2012–2017 were like a prolonged Black Friday, during which a small number of firms ended up spending over $60 billion buying up homes, whether they were foreclosed, distressed, or otherwise.[19] As John Christie, an executive at a clone of Invitation Homes, put it, "We recognized the unique opportunity created by the housing crisis and acted upon it in a bold way."[20]

By 2016, 95 percent of the distressed mortgages on Fannie Mae and Freddie Mac's books had been auctioned off to housing platforms like Invitation Homes.[21] By the 2020s, there were about 300,000 properties under investor management.[22] After several mergers, Invitation Homes became, by far, the largest.

What exactly made Invitation Homes a "platform," as opposed to just the owner of assets they hoped might appreciate? It is true that as the owner of the houses, Invitation was not a pure platform like, say, Airbnb. But it used many of the logistical techniques of the platform to manage the daunting prospects of houses as an asset. Houses had to be individually purchased, and then managed, maintained, rented, evicted, and re-rented. The logistics of doing that at scale were daunting. The answer was "technology," according to Greiwe. "We fundamentally believed we could use technology to enable a best-in-class team to identify, underwrite, purchase, renovate, and professionally lease/manage U.S. single-family rental homes across the country at scale." They built a "technology platform that didn't just become a useful tool; rather, it became existential to the success of our business."[23]

Invitation Homes and similar firms needed software to help buy thousands of homes a week. They came up with programs that identified target homes based on relevant data, such as projected value and maintenance costs, as well as neighborhood characteristics, like local school quality, crime, and proximity to transportation. They then semiautomated the buying process to make it work at scale.

To the credit of the new firms, buying the foreclosed homes in the early 2010s did help prevent the problem of foreclosed and abandoned "zombie homes" from becoming a blight on their communities. Greiwe, reflecting on his experience with Invitation Homes, writes that their goals included returns for investors, but also turning homes into "aesthetically pleasing, investment-grade assets that would ultimately attract renters."[24] If Invitation Homes had simply limited itself to the recovery of distressed assets, there would be little to criticize. However, the promises of oversized returns to investors forced the firms, over time, to turn to less agreeable tactics.

The initial plan had been for investors to merely flip foreclosed homes at scale and take the proceeds. But after some experience renting, and after a recovery in prices, the firms began to see holding on to the assets and renting at scale as a better model. This led Invitation Homes to turn to new and different strategies to increase profit.

The basic strategy has been simple: increase revenue and decrease costs. As for the former, the easiest source of more money has been systematic rent increases. Over the 2010s, during a period of limited inflation, Invitation Homes and other single-family-rental companies never missed a rent increase. Depending on the market, they aimed for between 7 to 13 percent in annual increases. That rate greatly exceeded inflation or average salary increases, creating financial challenges for poorer tenants. In an interview for a nonprofit, Maricela Castillo, a tenant in Sacramento, detailed how a rise in her rent from $1,200 to $1,600 over three years scrambled her family's finances. "The additional $400 a month—that cuts into our ability to feed my kids and meet our basic needs."[25]

Another strategy, borrowed from the airline and banking industries, was to maximize "ancillary income," a fancy word for fees. While fees are an annoyance for most of us, for scale businesses they are pure profit; and in the case of "junk fees,"[*] they are a handy way of hiding full prices. What's more, there is a turning point in the lives of most platforms (and many businesses) when they stop innovating in terms of quality and begin innovating in ways to cleverly charge more for the same product.

Invitation Homes turned the charging of fees into an art form. In addition to the usual application fees that are charged to prospective renters, they charged late fees ($95),[26] termination fees, and turnover fees. One innovation was a mandatory "utility management fee," which was later morphed into a "Lease Easy Bundle" fee, which includes the utility management fee, a further "air filter" fee, and a "smart home technology" (or "smart home") fee.[27] The $30 to $40 monthly "smart home" fee (allowing remote operation of locks and other features through an app) was initially optional, but became mandatory across the company soon after the CEO ordered management to "juice this hog."[28]

All these mandatory fees were in effect a means of increasing rents. But there was plenty to be gained in quasi-optional fees. Pet owners were charged a $325 deposit plus an additional monthly fee of $40 per pet at Invitation Homes, meaning that the owner of three cats was on the line for an extra $1,440 a year for the privilege of feline companionship.[29] The firm also made it a practice of seizing security deposits at the end of rentals, with the idea of forcing renters to sue to try to get them back. In one of many examples, a Nashville woman named Desiree Tromblee told the local news station that when she attempted to leave her Invitation Homes rental, she was charged both the full security deposit of $1,300 and an additional $7,600 in alleged damages (the fees were dropped after media attention).[30]

"Even little, tiny nickel-and-diming, if it's done across your entire portfolio, like little fees here and there—you can model those, you can predict those," writes Meredith Abood, who stud-

---

[*] The phrase "junk fees" is a colloquial term for the practices of either (1) mandatory fees that are disclosed later, and are effectively part of the price (like hotel "resort fees"), or (2) fees charged for little or nothing in return, or grossly unrelated to underlying costs (like overdraft fees).

ied the platform housing industry, "and then that can be a huge revenue source."[31] For Invitation Homes, the fees were adding tens of millions in profit to the bottom line. The Lease Easy bundle alone earned the firm $60 million from 2021 to 2023.

On the other side of the ledger, to keep costs low, over the 2010s, the firms put clear caps on repair costs and their own labor costs. All the firms are minimally staffed—at one firm, Starwood Homes, some 304 staff manage over 32,000 homes.[32] The firms have invested in efforts to both standardize maintenance and force tenants to do more repairs themselves. In fact, the leases promulgated by Invitation Homes and other firms tell tenants they are responsible for all nonmajor repairs, including repairs to appliances, plumbing, and windows. There is a near-unlimited supply of tenant complaints about the lack of repairs, even for major problems. In that context, the story that the Suszczewicz family in Phoenix told to a local news outlet is typical.[33] They moved into an Invitation house with a pool in north Phoenix, only to find a toilet leaking, another toilet inoperable, and the one accessible shower unable to run hot water. Those problems lasted for months. The worst part, said the Suszczewiczes, was that the promised pool was unusable for a full year—but they were nonetheless subject to a $90 per month "pool maintenance fee," adding up to more than a thousand dollars for an unusable pool. Another tenant, Celeste Jackson in Los Angeles, whose house was subject to rotting and leaking, said: "We're paying $4,000 a month to live in hell."[34]

The strategy of raising prices and cutting costs was quite successful for Invitation Homes. By the 2020s, now a publicly traded company, the firm was reporting a market value of over $20 billion,[35] and the platform-driven housing industry more broadly has experienced steady growth. The complaints and press coverage have indeed hurt the reputation of Invitation Homes; yet in a period of acute shortage of housing, some prospective tenants report that in some areas, all their options are corporate landlords. As one Reddit user said of Invitation Homes: "They have a stated business plan: buy up houses in lower-income communities, jack up rents, have a monopoly."[36] The deceptive fee structure did, however, catch the attention of the Federal Trade

Commission, which sued Invitation Homes and, in September 2024, forced it to return some $48 million in fees to its current and former tenants.[37]

There is a deeper structural significance to the centralization of real estate and housing as an asset class. Distributed ownership of real property has long been core to an American economic identity. As John Adams wrote in the founding era, "The balance of power in a society accompanies the balance of property in land. The only possible way, then, of preserving the balance of power on the side of equal liberty and public virtue, is to make the acquisition of land easy for every member of society."[38]

The centralization of housing control does the exact opposite of this. At the risk of stating the obvious, it drives a trend of centralizing property ownership away from the individual and the family and toward large owners.

To be sure, the trend is new and its broader significance unclear. The housing platforms are large fish (Invitation Homes holds about $19 billion in assets).[39] But they are in a very large pond, given that there are some 45 million rental units in the United States and the total estimated value of U.S. residential real estate is over $40 trillion.[40] Big things have small beginnings, however, and the spread of centralized home ownership is a big thing. At bottom, home ownership has been, for a long time, the bulwark of what remains of the "property-owning democracy" tradition in the American economy, as well as a major mechanism of forced savings. Changes to this structure are of foundational significance.

The transformation of the economy to one in which platform power has become central in tech and other industries shows signs of being the signal economic event of the last half century. This is not to deny the residual power in industrial production and the service economy. But in economies that are centered on platform organizations, such assets and capacities become dependent on the coordinating power.

The opportunity lies in the advantages of the platform model and what it makes possible, including the possibility of mobilizing a broad base of economic actors. The danger and downside are nothing to shrug off: it is the danger that centralized economic power and extraction naturally present. That includes the economic pitfalls but also severe political dangers as well, as the next part explores in depth.

PART III

THE DANGERS OF CENTRALIZED ECONOMIC POWER

If you haven't noticed, the twenty-first century has been a bit rocky, both economically and politically. The United States has weathered a Great Recession, an economic collapse and recovery during the COVID pandemic, and a lasting regional, class, and race-based inequality that has contributed to bitter political polarization and tribalism.

Around the world, matters are, if anything, even more unstable. Of the many new democracies born in the 1990s or early twenty-first century, more than twenty-five have returned either to dictatorship, like in Egypt and Thailand, or authoritarian semi-democracy, as in Hungary and Turkey.[1] China and Russia are once again ruled by autocrats. All around the world economic despair and disparity have yielded mass migrations that have disrupted both wealthy and poor nations.

It wasn't supposed to be this way. Not so long ago many were looking to the twenty-first century with a broad sense of optimism, reflected well in Francis Fukuyama's famous 1992 book *The End of History and the Last Man*.[2] He proclaimed that we were witnessing not just "the passing of a particular period of post-war history, but the end of history as such." We had reached "the end point of mankind's ideological evolution and the universalization of Western liberal democracy as the final form of human government." The old dictators, cranky old men, were on their way out. A kinder, gentler future was meant to be on its way in. Everyone would be both wealthy and free.

What went wrong? To borrow a phrase: it was the economy, stupid. Missing from the rosy story of the future was an appreciation of the destabilizing effects of laissez-faire capitalism, both within societies and internationally. And while the tech platforms are not nearly the entirety of this story, the rise of the extractive platform within the tech industries and across the economy has helped to centralize economic power in a manner that we have still not fully understood or appreciated. The goal of the third part of this book is to step back to understand the risks we are taking.

CHAPTER 11

ECONOMIC MANIA

Viewed over the longer run of history, the twenty-first century suffers from the same kind of economically driven political instability that haunted other periods of human history. When you get beneath the surface, the imbalances drove the oppressive social structures of past centuries, including feudalism, monopoly capitalism, Stalinism, and fascist command capitalism. The expression and manifestations are different, but our risk of meeting the same fate is real.

We should know by now that aggregating economic and political power in a few people or corporations is dangerous. Yet we also have a curious way of forgetting. On the way up, the aggregation of power can yield a manic high, one capable of convincing a nation that all its problems have been solved. Like a powerful stimulant, it blinds us to its dangers. In the late 1920s, unaware of what was coming, many in the West believed they had achieved endless prosperity and a materialist nirvana in the hands of the world's corporate captains. In the late 1930s, Stalin was hailed as an economic genius after he reorganized the Soviet economy along the lines of a giant corporation. In the 2000s, we became caught up in our own kind of high, fueled by cheap money, financial deregulation, corporate consolidation, and a strange faith that we could avoid what had befallen previous generations.

But history also tells us that there is a cycle and that over-centralization usually leads in two directions: a crash or long-term stagnation. At its worst, an economic system that hoards too much wealth in too few hands can inspire a violent revolution. To see just how badly things can go, let's look at the lessons that can be taken from what was once the wealthiest place in the Western Hemisphere. Here is the story of the Saint-Domingue colony.

As of the late 1770s, the Caribbean island of Saint-Domingue was widely envied for its wealth and export economy. On the eve of the American Revolution, the small island, a French colony, was booking exports roughly equivalent to those of all thirteen American colonies combined. By the 1780s, the "pearl of the Antilles" was producing about 40 percent of all the sugar and 60 percent of all the coffee consumed in Europe.[1] Following something close to today's corporate playbook, the economy focused on just a few profitable products, maximizing productivity through economies of scale and keeping costs—especially labor costs—as low as possible.

Scale was achieved through large and highly organized sugar and coffee plantations. "A sugar plantation was a factory set in a field," writes Richard Pares.[2] Labor costs were kept in check by a particularly savage brand of slavery. And by the most superficial of measures, it worked for the plantation owners—at least for a while.[3]

Unequal societies are always fragile, but Saint-Domingue was at an extreme. Over half a million Africans were ruled over by a small number of plantation owners, their lieutenants, and other staff.[4] The high rates of mortality among the enslaved, from yellow fever and other diseases, were estimated by one scholar to be 50 percent among the newly arrived, and 5 or 6 percent among the acclimatized.[5] Many plantation owners apparently did the math, making the grim calculation that importing new workers from Africa was more cost-effective than attempting to make work safer or otherwise decrease mortality rates.[6]

In August 1791, the enslaved workers of Saint-Domingue

rose in revolt. By one account, thousands attended a secret religious ceremony as a tropical storm came in: the thunder and lightning were viewed as auspicious omens. That same night, the former slaves began to burn the plantations, killing or capturing their former masters. We have the eyewitness account of the director of the Clément plantation, after being woken by noises: "I jumped out of my bed and shouted, 'Who goes there?' A voice like thunder answered me, 'It is death!'" The slave revolt plunged the colony into a civil war that lasted fourteen years.[7]

In 1804, the rebels finally took control of the island and declared independence, naming their new country Haiti ("the land of high mountains"). Haiti declared itself a free republic, abolished slavery for good, and conducted an island-wide massacre of most of the remaining Europeans.[8] But the island was devastated, by both the war and the legacy of slavery, and has never fully recovered. It would be further damaged economically by the reparations demanded by France (reparations not to the formerly enslaved but to their former owners, lasting until 1947 and at times representing as much as 80 percent of Haiti's revenue). The island that was once among the wealthiest places in the world is today the poorest in the Western Hemisphere.[9]

Haiti is an extreme example—so enormous were its economic and political imbalances. But the point is that *any* economic system can drift toward being like Saint-Domingue. Wealth and economic growth can be gained by tolerating economic imbalances, but at great risk. More generally, concentrated economies can gain output through specialization, scale, and coercive reduction of labor costs. But the downside is an inherent fragility that can yield catastrophic crashes.

This cycle repeats throughout modern history—growth and wealth achieved by economic centralization followed by terrifying crashes and chaos, and often the rise of a strongman. It would take another book to chronicle every example. Some of the major examples include the tsarist regime in Russia; the American, British, German, and Japanese industrial economies of the 1920s–30s; and the resource-wealthy economies of Central and South America, among many others.

Our platform economy obviously does not take the same

form as the monopolized capitalism of the early twentieth century and bears even less resemblance to slave colonies like Saint-Domingue. Yet we are on a trajectory that has created a concentrated and unfair economy with similar risks. In short, we are conducting a reckless economic experiment that history suggests has rarely gone well. Most dangerous of all, it has a track record of creating conditions conducive to the rise of an authoritarian strongman.

THE REAL ROAD TO SERFDOM

The real road to serfdom—to an authoritarian state—runs through the imbalance of economic power, and a platform economy contributes to that problem. What do I mean by the road to serfdom? The phrase comes from Austrian economist Friedrich Hayek, who believed that a well-meaning government, as it expanded and began to engage in centralized economic planning, was certain to metastasize into a despotic totalitarian state. But Hayek missed something important and essential: that failures of government can contribute to the flip to authoritarianism that he feared. Government can indeed be dangerous. But so can its absence.

Here is the sequence in five steps, each based on known and well-studied tendencies.

The first is *monopolization*—the takeover of the major industries in the economy by either actual monopolies or a small number of dominant firms. That outcome is the predictable result of unrestrained markets, populated by power- and profit-seeking corporations backed by finance. As William Magnuson puts it, "Corporations, by their nature, are constantly seeking to concentrate market power."

Of course, monopoly is a theoretical abstraction; the more common reality is the rise of firms with market power, whether they be a small number of dominant firms (a "big three") or the colonialization of local markets by foreign or distant firms. Regardless of the exact form, the signature of the monopolized economy is its power and ability to undertake the next stage: extraction.

The *extraction* stage is characterized by the division of the economy into winners and losers—the "two-class economy." Firms with market power enrich their owners and investors, top managers and their agents, including lawyers, bankers, and other professionals. By its nature, that creates a narrow class of winners, whether those rewarded with extraordinary incomes or the owners of capital who enjoy high rates of return and slow growth.

The losers are a broader class: consumers who pay more, workers who are paid less, and local, regional, smaller, and medium-sized businesses that are acquired or driven out of business. The divide can be geographic, with entire regions or countries left behind, providing low-return inputs with a minimal share of profit. The extraction stage can take subtle forms, especially in developed countries—represented, for example, by the careful finding of pockets of market power, such as those around a patented drug, nursing homes, or the surprise pricing of medical services.

The third step, following and accompanying systemic extraction, is the *emergence of mass resentment*. There will always be some level of economic dissatisfaction in any country, but broad-based resentment is something different. As Robert Schneider details in his 2023 book *The Return of Resentment*, it is a political emotion that arises from a de-enrichment of large groups based on location, class, tribe, or race.[10] It is a sorting of society along lines having little to do with one's individual abilities and is inhumane in that sense. The expression of grievance may consist of blaming scapegoats, like immigrants, ethnic or religious minorities, or greedy elites.

The fourth step is *democratic failure*. It is where an elected government is either unable or unwilling to respond to majority resentment in a meaningful way. The failure is compounded if the state is understood or credibly portrayed as supporting and perpetuating the ongoing extraction, perhaps to its own advantage, the problem better known as corruption. This is a key turning point, for those enriched by the extraction stage will seek to prevent any action and thereby cause democratic failure.

Democratic failure leads to the *rise of the strongman*, who offers an apparently credible commitment to respond to unaddressed resentment and grievance. The strongman's popularity always lies in a promise to truly serve the interests of the people. Some actually do—at least for a while, as in the early days of Mussolini, Hugo Chavez, Muammar Gaddafi, and many other such figures. But over the longer term, the track record of authoritarian dictators leaves much to be desired. They are the figures who turn the slow road to serfdom into an expressway.

This is the sequence. The question is how to break it.

CHAPTER 12

SOME SOLUTIONS

And what's your system of belief, Olivia?
Not capitalism; not socialism. So just cynicism?

—NICOLE MOSSBACHER in *White Lotus*

We have lived through the rise of an unbalanced economic system thanks to both the emergence of platform capitalism and broader trends in the economy. Given that fact, the challenge for our economic future is one of rebalancing economic power.

How can we build an economic architecture structured to deliver lasting prosperity for a broad population, as opposed to enrichment of one class or one group at the expense of others? It is certainly not easy, and some may think such a thing impossible. But it is not. We have, at times, had something like it in this country. Across the course of human history, there have existed economies that have not been dominated by monopolies or a single extractive class, achieving some relative level of economic equality. There are models to which we can aspire, and we will discuss them here.

We can put this into context by discussing the main previous forms of economic power—land and industrial power—and how successful civilizations managed the balance.

LAND

For much of recorded history, the principal source of economic power was land combined with human labor. The writings of early economists like Adam Smith and David Hume simply assume that arable land was the source of productivity. It is obvious that land ownership can be more or less centralized. At one extreme is the feudal economy, where land belongs to a small number of feudal lords, and where the peasants or serfs (sometimes slaves) have limited economic rights and are attached—by law—to the land itself. Almost by definition, feudal economies were unbalanced and unfair. They were not particularly productive either.

The reforms that most successfully broke feudalism were the land reforms that ended serfdom and—critically—gave peasants legal ownership or tenancy of the land they worked (or made it easy to acquire). Many of the most broadly prosperous nations practiced some version of land reform at the right moment, including seventeenth-century England, early nineteenth-century Scandinavia, and Japan, Korea, and Taiwan after the Second World War.

Let's spend a moment on the early United States, which in the North practiced a different variation of land reform—handing out free or highly subsidized land to immigrants. The early reputation of the northern United States as an equalitarian place was anchored in its broad distribution of land ownership. Alexis de Tocqueville was struck by "the general equality of condition among the people" in the 1830s. Founder and second president John Adams wrote that "the balance of power in a society accompanies the balance of property in land. The only possible way, then, of preserving the balance of power on the side of equal liberty and public virtue, is to make the acquisition of land easy to every member of society."

In fits and starts, but across administrations, the early northern and western states offered immigrant families cheap land on very good terms, an approach that was very different from that of the American South and most of South America. In a series of Land Acts passed between 1796 and 1820, the U.S. government offered eligible buyers 320 acres for $1.25 an acre and allowed repayment over four years. For a small down payment, one could own a sizable farm in what is now Michigan or Ohio. From these origins came a strong American middle class.

Occurring over roughly the same period, the story of Denmark makes for a particularly vivid example of the difference land reform can make. Today, Denmark is among the wealthiest and most equalitarian nations on earth. As Francis Fukuyama wrote: "Denmark is a mythical place that is known to have good political and economic institutions: it is stable, democratic, peaceful, prosperous, and inclusive."

But once upon a time—during the course of the American Revolution—the Kingdom of Denmark was the exact opposite of what it is today. It was poor and backward, ruled by an autocratic king, and economically dominated by a small number of manor lords who had doubled down on feudalism when others were giving it up. The lords owned an estimated 98 to 99 percent of the arable land, and by 1733, a decree known as the *Stavnsbånd* had bound peasants to the land of their birth until the age of thirty-six years old.[1] This was at a time when life expectancy in the country was roughly thirty-three years.

The feudal system was obviously bad for the peasants, but it wasn't great for the country either. Danish farming was unproductive. The peasants, "oppressed by the prevailing hierarchical institutional arrangements and discouraged by a depressing psychological and physical environment [. . .] had little incentive and slight ability to increase production."[2]

Denmark's transformation began in 1784 when a new ruler, Frederick, assumed the full powers of prince regent. At just nineteen years old, the new Prince Frederick liked the idea of ruling as an "enlightened monarch." In the royal version of John F. Kennedy's first one hundred days, he went big early on. He did so with the help of an advisor and de facto prime minister named Andreas Peter Bernstorff. It so happened that Bernstorff, as a young man, had become deeply devoted to physiocratic ideals of land reform and giving peasants ownership of the land they toiled.* Earlier in his life he had transformed his family's estate

---

* The physiocrats were a group of eighteenth-century economic thinkers who venerated farming and agricultural production, the Enlightenment's own "back to the land" move-

into an experiment in peasant ownership, and had managed to triple the production of rye and oats. As a young man, he wrote to his father: "It is unbelievable how their work and industriousness has increased since they became the proprietors of their own land."[3]

In 1788, the crown prince signed a decree, engineered by Bernstorff, that dramatically reformed the laws concerning agricultural land and made all of Denmark not unlike that experimental farm. The *Stavnsbånd* was abolished, freeing the peasants. In its place, the farmers were made into tenants and granted a series of legal protections against the lords. A new, state-backed loan program encouraged peasants to buy the land they had farmed. And over the next decade, tens of thousands of peasants were converted from bonded serfs into small landowners.

The short- and long-term effects of the land reforms were dramatic and nothing short of transformative in the direction they took the country economically and politically. In the short term, the nation's agricultural sector became vastly more productive. The production of grain increased some 40 percent, enabling Denmark to become a net exporter of grain. The number of cattle increased from 280,000 to 560,000. By setting off a small agricultural revolution, the reforms ended up benefiting both the former lords and the peasants.[4]

Over the longer term, the peasants themselves became a powerful political force, and the Danish people's embrace of small-scale production has persisted. Their farmers, resistant to consolidation, turned to the cooperative form in the late nineteenth century to achieve scale in meat and dairy production. The core of present-day Denmark's persistent middle class remains linked to the class of small landowners created by land reform.

Of course, none of this happened overnight or even linearly. Denmark had a rough time of it during the Napoleonic Wars. Fearing that Denmark might join France, in 1807 the British navy preemptively attacked Copenhagen, leading to fires that

---

ment. They were among the first to systematically challenge the ideas of the mercantilists, by insisting that national wealth came from productive labor—in particular, agricultural labor.

burnt down much of the city. It also hit hard economic times in the 1830s. Crown Prince Frederick, if a teenage idealist, became a more authoritarian figure later in life. The perfect state does not exist.

But there is a strong contrast between Denmark and similarly situated nations that failed to reform land ownership over the same period. The closest comparison from the same era is Russia. As in Denmark, eighteenth-century Russia had an economy centered on a class of manor lords who had held on to feudalism longer than the Western European states. Like Denmark, Russia had a leader—Empress Catherine—who considered herself an enlightened monarch dedicated to bringing her country into modern times. Coming to power in 1762, she would write (of herself), "When she came to the throne of Russia, she wished to do what was good for her country and tried to bring happiness, liberty, and prosperity to her subjects."[5]

But when it came to abolishing serfdom, Catherine whiffed. Early in her reign, in the 1760s, she drafted a secret law that would have slowly ended serfdom and reformed land ownership. But unlike in Denmark, her advisors were staunchly opposed, fearing "axioms which will bring down walls."[6] Not only was the plan never enacted—it was never even seen by anyone other than a very small group.

After failing to act early on, Catherine's reformist spirit began to fade. Her embrace of the Enlightenment became channeled in more aesthetic and personal directions, such as her effort to build a world-class art collection (now found in the Hermitage in Saint Petersburg) and her cultivation of relationships with various celebrities of the French Enlightenment, especially Voltaire. Meanwhile, during her reign the feudal economy became more restrictive and centralized. Under her watch, the buying and selling of serfs as human chattel became normalized. She agreed to laws that further limited the economic freedom of serfs, including laws requiring the landowner's permission for serfs to marry. She also gave up on an earlier effort to limit how landowners punished their serfs. As an older Catherine stated flatly, Russian serf owners "were free to do in their estates whatever seemed best to them, except to give the death penalty."[7]

The failure of Catherine and her successors to change the economic structure of feudal Russia took an economic and political toll. Economists Ekaterina Zhuravskaya and Andrei Markevich concluded, based on their analysis of nineteenth-century agricultural data, that "serfdom was a crucial factor causing a slowdown of economic development of Eastern Europe [. . .] that the difference in timing of the abolition of serfdom is an important reason for the divergence of development paths across the European continent."[8]

The longer-term political consequences were also disastrous. Russia finally abolished serfdom in 1861 and implemented a weak form of land reform, but it was too little, too late. The reforms did not forestall the violent Russian Revolution of 1905, or the even bloodier Soviet Revolution of 1917 and subsequent civil war. As we have repeatedly suggested, economically unbalanced countries are unstable. Had Russia or Catherine somehow managed to rebalance the economy and give land to the peasants earlier, there is reason to think the course of Russian history would have been different and might have involved considerably less violence and suffering.

INDUSTRIAL POWER

Let us now consider the second major source of raw economic power: industry. Industrial power arises primarily from scale, specialization, and ownership of productive assets. Manufacturing is its archetype, in firms like U.S. Steel, General Motors, Germany's Krupp, and Japan's Mitsubishi conglomerate. Over the early twentieth century, industrial power became concentrated among the owners of these kinds of large manufacturing facilities, leading to economic imbalance. How this power came to be balanced in some ways forms a main economic narrative of the twentieth century.

America's struggle with industrial power involves the growth of the anti-monopoly movement and the recognition of industrial unions. Let us instead tell the parallel story, in Europe, of the German industrial empires like Krupp and IG Farben.

These were among the world's largest firms in the early twentieth century—by 1938, Krupp had more than 210,000 workers. As Terence Prittie writes: for companies like Krupp, initially excluded from political power, a "concentration on economic power became single-minded, all-absorbing, remorseless" over the early twentieth century.[9]

The story of German monopoly owes much more to the cartel form—and the state. From the 1890s onward, the German government encouraged industry cartelization and consolidation. In other words, the state encouraged competing companies to work together to set prices, production quantities, quality standards, and so on. These eventually evolved into industrial monopolies, while German economists and intellectuals promoted such German-style monopolization as progressive and scientific. Prominent economic historian Gustav von Schmoller championed the *kartellen* as "a new order of public life." The German cartels were also the subject of national pride: many saw their industrial leaders as engaged in a fight against British, French, and American companies for Germany's fair share of the imperialist spoils.

Unrestrained and indeed spurred on by the state, Krupp, IG Farben, and other German firms were openly encouraged to monopolize their sectors in the latter days of the Weimar Republic. We have said that the aggregation of economic power can be very dangerous. In the case of Germany, after a terrible economic crash in 1930 leading to widespread misery and prolonged political chaos, Germany's main industrialists over the 1930s would come to support Hitler's rise to power as "the lesser of two evils." As one organizer of industry put it: "The general aim of the industrialists at that time, was to see a strong leader come to power in Germany who could form a government which would long remain in power."[10] The cartels, which had become full monopolies over the 1920s, formed the backbone of the Third Reich command economy, with consequences so horrific that they need not be elaborated on.

Let us discuss how industrial power was rebalanced in Germany and the United States. In the United States, as stated above, the two most successful tools were the anti-monopoly laws and the union movement. The former broke up most of its monopoly trusts in the 1900s through 1910s. Meanwhile, American unions, despite many setbacks over the early twentieth century, managed by the 1950s to grow into a power capable of balancing the largest corporations.

Germany did not have an anti-monopoly law, and its labor movement was crushed by the Nazi Party. The main monopolies, like Krupp and IG Farben, were allied with the Nazi state. The economic balancing was accomplished, therefore, by military defeat. After the fall of the Third Reich, the occupying forces launched a deliberate and aggressive economic program to reduce the concentrated power of German industry, known as "de-cartelization." A postwar Senate report explained the program this way: "The structure and control of German industry must be so altered [. . .] to crush German imperialism permanently and thus permit a peaceful and democratic Germany to arise."[11] To that end, the Allies imposed Rule 56, an anti-monopoly law designed to eliminate all "concentrations of economic power [. . .] which could be used by Germany as instruments of political or economic aggression."[12] The Allies broke up the major cartels and also encouraged the new German state to develop its own anti-monopoly law. A number of Krupp's and IG Farben's executives were also tried and convicted of war crimes, which included the use of slave labor, concentration camp labor, and the murder of enslaved persons.

Rising out of the ashes of the Nazi regime and with its main firms broken up, West Germany had, for an industrial power, a decentralized economy. There is more than one reason for Germany's nearly 8 percent per annum growth rate over the 1950s and its 4.6 percent growth through the 1960s—which increased the GDP by two-thirds and pushed the unemployment rate from 10.3 to 1.2 percent. But as Horst Siebert writes in *The German Economy: Beyond the Social Market*, de-cartelization and the subsequent increases in competition in the economy played an important role in recovery. Whatever else happened, West Germany did not suffer from the monopoly problems that had afflicted Germany and its politics earlier in the century.[13]

A final short example of a nation overcoming a very unpromising start comes from Asia and the island nation of Taiwan. As with the others, Taiwan was not—circa 1945—a likely prospect for balanced economic development. It had been a Japanese colony and was left, after the war, with a shattered infrastructure and a new government (from Nationalist China) that, at least at first, had opted to maintain the colonial economic structure. But facing pressure from the United States (which feared a communist uprising), the Taiwanese government pursued aggressive land reform—by one estimate, more than one million Taiwanese families gained property rights under the land reform program.[14] Later, as opposed to building up the colonial firms into industrial national champions, Taiwan instead gave broad license for entrepreneurialism and small production, the so-called *lao-ban* (small boss) economy. While Taiwan has a few well-known firms (like TSMC, the Taiwan Semiconductor Manufacturing Company), its small and medium business sector dominates the economy, making up 97 percent of business and employing nearly 80 percent of the workforce.

Taiwan—whose per capita GDP now exceeds Japan's—is among the strongest demonstrations of the fact that a country can grow rapidly without enduring enormous disparities in wealth and income. As economist John Fei and coauthors write in *Growth with Equity: The Taiwan Case:* "Two of Taiwan's achievements in the years after 1953 are particularly notable: extremely rapid rates of economic growth were accompanied by improvements in the family distribution of income; [while] unemployment, or under-employment, was virtually eliminated." The idea that growth cannot happen without enriching a narrow class is a self-perpetuating myth.

These examples—of feudal Denmark, the fascist command economy of Nazi Germany, and colonial Taiwan—show that it is possible to balance even what might seem like the most hopelessly unbalanced economic system. It does not happen without deliberate action, but once the structure is built and anchored with a strong institution like property rights, countries can remain balanced for some time. Examples include the northern United

States post-revolution and from the FDR period through the 1970s; the modern Nordic countries, Taiwan, Japan, and Korea after World War II; and according to a new wave of scholars, the ancient Greek city-states. None are perfect—there has never been an ideal state, and there may never be one. But we should move forward by gathering the best of what has worked, by collecting up the pieces that represent what we should aspire to.

In this view, the great societies are not those that get big and then crash and burn, even if they may be entertaining to read about. Rather, they are the societies that managed to deliver on a promise of opportunity and prosperity for long stretches of time. They delivered by creating significant work and property ownership for much of their populations and, above all, providing enough economic security and leisure so that life might be enjoyed rather than merely endured. These are societies with economies that feel fair. As Justice Louis Brandeis once said, "the 'right to life'" should be understood as "the right to live, and not merely to exist."[15]

CHAPTER 13

THE PERSISTENT DREAM OF THE SELF-CORRECTING ECONOMY

Despite a track record of crashes and suffering, it has long been the belief of some economists that unrestrained markets can solve any problems by themselves, including imbalances of economic power. Any dangerous level of market power can be expected to dissipate naturally; any monopolies, like the tech platforms discussed in this book, will have a power that is fleeting and temporary. This is the theory of self-correcting markets. Given the observed persistence of monopoly in our times, you may think this theory so implausible as to not be worth reading about, and if so, you can skip the chapter. But you should at least know that it has had an enormous influence over economic policy for more than a century.

The theory of self-correcting markets depends on an assumption that economies behave like the systems of dynamic equilibrium found in nature, particularly in biology, where they are referred to as homeostatic systems. In human biology, there are many self-correcting systems that do react to imbalances. For example, our bodies maintain an internal temperature of about

37°C / 98°F, even if we walk outside on a cold day.* The theory is that markets behave the same way: they automatically react to and correct imbalances, and return to a healthy equilibrium.

What gives the theory legs is that economic systems—markets—do have observable tendencies that inspire the comparison. If someone is standing on a street corner on a hot day making money selling water, odds are someone else will head out there and try their luck. The most important self-correcting tendency is that of large and undefended profits to attract new firms into a market. That observation yielded a belief (first advanced in the 1870s) that markets will detect deviations from an ideal state and self-correct to fix it.

Based as it is on natural science, the hypothesis has both an intuitive and an aesthetic appeal, and it has captivated thinkers for more than a century and a half. That said, the most obvious defect is this: it assumes that a firm, once having gained a monopoly, will not or cannot defend its position. That assumption is counterintuitive, given the propensity of humans to defend what they believe to be theirs. Would we really expect a firm, having built up its position over the years, to surrender it so easily? Even our humble corner water seller might take whatever measures she can to defend a profitable perch. If so, just how self-correcting will the market be? Might it get stuck, instead, in an unhealthy equilibrium?

Those might seem like important points to consider, yet the theory of perfectly self-correcting markets has hung on with an extraordinary tenacity. Consider three famous examples from the intellectual history of economics and how they have fared.

The first is the theory of "perfect competition," originating with David Ricardo but expressed most clearly by price economists of the late nineteenth century like Alfred Marshall, who wrote and released the influential *Principles of Economics* in 1890. Marshall and other economists theorized that markets should generally be expected to "clear" and reach a "partial equilibrium,"

---

* It is also the case that extreme conditions can overcome a biological equilibrium and require external intervention. For example, a man dropped into the Arctic Ocean will find his rebalancing systems overcome within a few minutes.

in which firms set their price near their cost of production (known as the competitive price). As we detailed above, it assumed that anyone who starts earning a big profit, or a monopoly profit, will face competitors who see that profit as a lure and leap to seize it themselves.*

Astonishingly, Marshall and his followers theorized perfect competition in the midst of the monopoly movement of the late nineteenth and early twentieth centuries. The greatest faith in the unstoppable power of competitive forces coincided with their absence. The great profits of monopolies like Standard Oil and the Tobacco Trust were not seized by competitors. Instead, men like John Rockefeller and Andrew Carnegie became the wealthiest men in human history at the expense of smaller business units and workers, and almost at the expense of the American republic.

Somehow the growth and persistence of monopoly did not shake the theory's influence. That is, until the Great Depression hit and took Marshall's perfect competition with it. The failure of the economy to return to equilibrium and the work of John Maynard Keynes undermined it.† More economists began to assert that the classic theory of perfect competition was not descriptive of the actual economy. Economists like Joan Robinson and Edward Chamberlin argued that imperfect competition or monopoly was the norm and that in reality, Marshall's perfect competition was a rarity. Even Joseph Schumpeter would write that for most markets, "there seems to be no reason to expect to yield the results of perfect competition," and that "in the general case of oligopoly there is in fact no determinate equilibrium at all."[1]

Yet with a stubborn persistence, the theory of self-correction returned in a different form in the 1950s, most notably, in John Kenneth Galbraith's theory of "countervailing power," found in *American Capitalism* (1952). Galbraith did not bother to defend the theory of perfect competition. He believed that many indus-

---

* To give the theory its due, there are situations where something close to such "perfect" competition can, and does, occur. The best example is in agricultural commodities such as wheat or corn. Marshall and classical economists took such markets as the rule and deviations as the exception.

† During the Depression, aggregate demand remained stubbornly stuck at low levels, despite the prediction of classic economics that demand would rise to meet supply.

tries would be dominated by a small number of large corporations, firms like General Motors and U.S. Steel. Galbraith also
accepted that such aggregations of power could create serious
economic problems, such as the driving down of wages and influence over politics.

But Galbraith said not to worry, based on a new theory of
market self-correction. He predicted that the great economic
power of corporations would be automatically matched by a
growing "countervailing power" in adjacent parts of the economy, like the suppliers of raw materials or labor. "As a common
rule," he wrote, "we can rely on countervailing power to appear
as a curb on economic power." In particular, he predicted that
any growth in corporate power would automatically be met by a
growth in union power. In 1952, he wrote: "As a general though
not invariable rule one finds the strongest unions in the United
States where markets are served by strong corporations."[2]

The theory of countervailing power is important, but as we
can see, Galbraith's predictions have not aged well. At the time
he was writing, in the 1950s, more than 30 percent of the private
U.S. workforce was unionized, and large manufacturers were balanced by large corporations. So, at that one moment—with that
one set of data points—his theory looked good. But over the last
forty years, despite rising corporate power, unionization has not
risen to match. Rather, private-sector unionization has continued
a long decline, reaching about 6 percent by 2023.[3]

Things get worse for Galbraith when you look at individual
firms and industries. The tech industry, home to many of the
strongest corporations in the United States, is almost entirely
nonunionized.[*] The largest and most profitable firms, including
Walmart, Amazon, and Apple, have little or no checks on their
power as employers. Meanwhile, there is little evidence that the
power of sellers of other inputs has matched rising firm power.
Instead, the squeezing of suppliers has become a constant complaint in the platform economy.

American Capitalism does nonetheless make a very important

---

* There is a Google employee union, but as of the mid-2020s, it comprises less than 1 percent of the company's workforce.

contribution: it tells us why we need countervailing power in the economy. We will return to countervailing power in Part IV. But the notion that it can be expected to automatically dissipate market power is just nonsense.

A third major variant comes from the work of the influential theorist Simon Kuznets. A pioneer of empirical methods, Kuznets was also a theorist of inequality, and among his postulates was the idea that unequal societies would, if they kept growing, automatically become equal again.* His work became a license for nations to focus on generating growth and wealth only, based on the premise that the accumulated, concentrated wealth would eventually trickle down to everyone else. The market economy was like the Cat in the Hat—whatever mess it might make, it would automatically clean up later.

Wouldn't that be nice? But like the other theories surveyed here, when tested, it failed. That was shown in the work of French economist Thomas Piketty, who used the same data as Kuznets but expanded the time horizon. After the 1960s and 1970s, inequality, which had been suppressed by two world wars and the Great Depression, began to grow again. The belief that increased wealth would naturally lead to greater equality, Piketty wrote, was a "fairy tale."[4]

In each of these cases, we see the same phenomenon. While competitive forces help dissipate dangerous levels of market power, it does not always automatically disappear and can, in fact, even continue to increase. What went wrong?

Examined more carefully, what each theory misses or omits is the same: the theory of self-correcting economic power routinely ignores the predictable actions of those who have that economic power. The great monopolists are not passive: they actively defend their market position by buying out dangerous competitors, controlling access to business essentials, diminishing unions, and enlisting the assistance of government. That's the

---

* To Kuznets's credit, he was modest about his conclusion, admitting that "[n]o adequate empirical evidence is available for checking this conjecture," and suggesting that "[t]he paper is perhaps 5 percent empirical information and 95 percent speculation, some of it possibly tainted by wishful thinking."

easiest explanation for why the theories fail: they do not account for the assertion of economic power to preserve that economic power. To change the metaphor one more time, they are like a physics of motion that ignores Newton's third law.

The error is so common that it might be given a name—the "passive monopolist fallacy." In reality, as any businessman knows, firms do everything they can to prevent losing market power—in business lingo, building "moats" and "walls" consisting of switching costs, brand loyalty, network effects, and governmental regulation. And why not? Market power is money *and* power, two things that most firms want.

Why the economic prophets surveyed here decided to ignore such countervailing forces is a good question for a cultural historian. Unshakable faith in market equilibrium has a special power to muddy clear thinking. For the theory of self-correcting markets can convince many an intelligent person that a return to a healthy equilibrium must always be around the corner, whatever the present circumstances look like, and however long that long run may be.*

The better view takes it as folly to hope that the dangers of market power will always dissipate naturally or to assume that because any problem will disappear "in the long run" it can be neglected now. That is not to say that self-correcting tendencies do not exist. It is, rather, to say that those tendencies are just tendencies, not laws of economic destiny.

While this discussion of self-correcting markets might seem academic, it has essential implications for economic policy. For a belief in long-run self-correction gives license to ignore the dangers of unbridled capitalism, based always on the premise that eventually, the problem will fix itself. It takes the position of the doctor who declines to treat a patient in the belief that the human body will always, in the end, reach or return to equilibrium. It may well, but the patient might also suffer terribly or die along the way.

---

* As economist Jean Charles Léonard Simonde de Sismondi wrote, "A certain kind of equilibrium, it is true, is reestablished in the long run, but it is after a frightful amount of suffering." Keynes's line is more famous: "In the long run we are all dead."

This is also not to overlook the dangers of state power and its exercise. To borrow from Galbraith: every aggregation of power needs to be balanced. As bad as assuming an infallible market may be, assuming an infallible state is even worse. That was of course the key error made by Karl Marx and his followers. While this is not a book about the failures of the communist economies, it is worth noting that twentieth-century Marxist-Leninist economies actually embraced the same program of centralization of economic power as the capitalists did. At its height, the Soviet Union was organized like an overgrown American corporation, with Joseph Stalin as its CEO. Instead of firing people, he had them shot or sent them to Siberia. Hence, as implemented, Marxism-Leninism offered no truly structural alternative to monopoly capitalism.

We've discussed some of the classic debates over centralized economic power. But what about technological answers? Might artificial intelligence, or cryptocurrency, make an unfair world economy fairer?

CHAPTER 14

ARTIFICIAL INTELLIGENCE AND CRYPTO: THE TECHNOLOGICAL ANSWERS TO ECONOMIC INEQUALITY

Sam Altman is best known as the CEO and leader of OpenAI, but he also considers himself a significant backer of progressive causes, including the problems of inequality and global poverty. He is a believer in Universal Basic Income (UBI, a guaranteed monthly stipend for all individuals), and he has helped secure funding for UBI experiments in California. In 2019, he cofounded a company named Tools for Humanity, meant to develop technological solutions for some of the economic challenges facing the world. Tools for Humanity, or TFH, casually raised a few hundred million dollars and spent a few years working on a secret project. In October 2023, it went public with something called the Worldcoin, meant to be a remedy for inequality. As the company explained in a press release:[1]

> Grand challenges in the next decade are global income inequality, governance of existential risks, and distinguishing humans from artificial intelligence. Humanity needs a protocol to solve these challenges. Worldcoin aims to be this protocol [. . .] with World ID.

World ID aims to be a unique identification system for humanity—like a global driver's license—that relies on unique biometric data. How exactly does it get that data? Well, that is where the large silver orbs come in.

Worldcoin, soon after launch, unveiled the Orb—a custom-made, portable iris scanner embedded in a shiny sphere about the size of a bowling ball. After manufacturing several thousand Orbs, the firm sent out operators tasked with scanning as many irises as possible and signing up people using the Orb. Each scan entitled the new member to twenty-five Worldcoins—said to be worth as much as fifty dollars at one point, though somewhat difficult to convert into hard currency. The promise of free money was attractive enough that by late 2024, Worldcoin claimed nearly 7 million members with scanned IDs.

You might ask what scanning eyeballs has to do with saving the world from economic unfairness. Worldcoin has been, in theory, hoping to create a robust identity system that could serve to help people prove their humanity. Based on that building block, it would therefore aim to serve as the foundation for building what it calls "a more human economic system." Or, as the firm puts it: "Worldcoin aims to provide universal access to the global economy no matter your country or background, establishing a place for all of us to benefit in the age of AI."*

That's the theory, anyhow, which includes an awful lot of hand-waving and depends on many, many things going right. But as critics have pointed out, there's also something else blindingly obvious going on. Data is valuable, and Worldcoin can also be understood as a company with a lot of investor money vacuuming up lots of data—in this case, biometric data, some of the most valuable of all. The Orbs were, in their own way, extraction machines, even if Worldcoin states that it intends to give "ownership to everyone."

---

* From the Worldcoin Whitepaper: "Using World ID, individuals will be able to prove that they are a real, unique human to any platform that integrates with the protocol. This will enable fair airdrops, provide protection against bots/Sybil attacks on social media, and enable the fairer distribution of limited resources. Furthermore, World ID can also enable global democratic processes and novel forms of governance (e.g., via quadratic voting), and it may eventually support a path to AI-funded UBI."

Worldcoin hasn't done much but scan irises yet, but its story captures something significant about the gaps between some of the aspirations and the reality of technological answers to global economic challenges, especially using AI or crypto technologies. Between the two, the AI solutions to economic challenges of the future are actually even more vague and unbaked than those centered on crypto. (Altman, as discussed in the introduction, merely asserts that generalized AI will eliminate global poverty.) At least crypto was meant as a counter to centralized economic power. So, leaving AI to one side, let's seriously consider the question: What role might blockchain or cryptocurrencies play in any effort to rebalance the economy?

If the great tech platforms have been forces of centralization, crypto is, in theory, a counterweight, and a force of decentralization. Over the last fifteen years, beginning with Bitcoin, people have used blockchains with the explicit goal of decentralizing economic institutions—and Bitcoin's multitrillion-dollar valuation indicates at least some success in that regard.

Yet at the same time, the crypto movement has struggled to avoid its own centralization and has also been plagued by theft, scams, ridiculously overhyped projects, and repeated sagas of young men overcome by greed and self-delusion. That said, it has also made a fairly large number of people some decent money and is constantly both overrated and underrated at the same time. Let's take a closer look.

CRYPTO'S PROMISE

It all begins with Bitcoin, the most successful digital currency of the twenty-first century. With more than a touch of the anarchist's instinct, Bitcoin was created in the late 2000s by a secretive man, Satoshi Nakamoto, who may be a real person but who might also merely be a mystical personification, like Tony the Tiger or the Marlboro Man. Launching in early 2009, Bitcoin was designed to be difficult or impossible to control and also difficult to mint. A core idea is a reliance on code as opposed to humans or human institutions. The limit of 21 million mineable coins cannot be adjusted, and there is no way to "print Bitcoin" in the manner that a state might print money.

Let's examine how the broader adoption of Bitcoin would decentralize capitalism in a best-case scenario. A long-standing and critical theory of banking—as popular in the 1790s as it is today—holds that banking systems, including national banks, are inherently political creations that favor certain economic actors. As well described by Charles W. Calomiris and Stephen H. Haber in *Fragile by Design* (2015), the political nature of banking systems means that they cannot avoid helping some industries and hurting others. The government, as it needs access to credit itself, is also heavily dependent on banks. Hence, the direction of money will always be toward favored industries. That contributes to fragility and crashes, the need for bailouts, and the inevitable pressures to carry out macroeconomic objectives despite a pretense of neutrality.

A money system that is separate from the government, according to this theory, would be less prone to political manipulation and favoritism. It might be a noninflationary and nonfluctuating currency that remains independent of any industry, tribe, or political group, and neutral between uses.

The mysterious creators of Bitcoin were not secretive about their ambition to be just such a currency. The creation of Bitcoin was widely understood as a reaction to the financial crisis of the late 2000s and, in particular, the conduct of the Federal Reserve and Bank of England. As crypto enthusiasts well know, hidden within the very first Bitcoin record was the message: "The Times, Jan 3, 2009: 'Chancellor on brink of second bailout for banks.'"[*]

There are actually many in the crypto world who see their goal as reducing global wealth inequality. Dunstan Teo, the cofounder of Philcoin (a blockchain-based philanthropy proj-

---

[*] Other currencies and blockchains, of which Ethereum is the best-known example, take these concepts further. The inventors and believers in blockchains think they could be used to decentralize a broad range of institutions or functions. What those functions could be, exactly, is sometimes left a bit vague. It seems pretty clear that you can't use blockchain to replace the fire department. But things like insurance contracts, financial derivatives, gambling, cloud storage, or digital identification could be accomplished with blockchain, or otherwise be tokenized in some manner.

ect), argued that crypto products "reduce income inequality by giving anyone, anywhere in the world, access to the same financial products. [. . .] Quite simply, crypto levels the playing field for all."[2] We already mentioned Worldcoin, cofounded by the well-known OpenAI developer Sam Altman. Worldcoin wants to "ingrain humanness and financial equitability in the global digital infrastructure," by "giving ownership to everyone." As you may recall, to accomplish this, Altman's firm developed those specialized cameras embedded in shiny balls. The idea was to create a robust digital identity to make global commerce easier for the world's poor. Or, as the company says, it "aims to provide universal access to the global economy no matter your country or background, establishing a place for every human to benefit."[3]

We now have the promise, more or less. Unspoken but always implicit is the possibility that the poor and unbanked of the world (or maybe just middle-class tech geeks) might manage to latch onto an asset that is appreciating and rebalance wealth that way. Bitcoin has already in its own way created wealth for those who were willing to buy it in the early days. One theory is that Bitcoin and crypto reward those willing to be a bit unconventional, leaving establishment sticks-in-the-mud with smaller returns.

Unlike many of my colleagues and friends, I do not see the whole crypto movement as just a complicated pyramid scheme. Unfortunately, crypto's founders have a bad habit of proving the detractors right, as various episodes over the last ten years tend to suggest.

THE YOUNGMAN PROBLEM

Back in the very early years of Bitcoin—circa 2010 or so—it was truly decentralized, but also nearly valueless. It was easy to generate, or "mine," using a regular computer. Some hapless geek spent 10,000 Bitcoin in 2010 ordering two pizzas—spending what is now nearly half a billion dollars by present value.[4]

Bitcoin was freely available to anyone willing to devote computing resources to mine the stuff—in other words, willing to leave a computer running all day and night to solve complex math problems. Setting up a mining rig wasn't easy, but it wasn't impossible, either—very doable for hobbyists. At least in theory, mining was open to anyone with time, patience, and decent computing skills. Some of those who mined it and avoided spending the proceeds on pizza or weed managed to make good money.

The mechanisms for buying and selling Bitcoin were also, in the early days, extraordinarily decentralized. Buyers and sellers would find each other on online forums, like Craigslist or Reddit, and would meet in person to exchange cash for Bitcoin. There was no matchmaking exchange, and no automatic way for buyers to find sellers. There was also no conclusive way to figure out what the prevailing price should be. It was not unlike the exchange of trading comics or baseball cards, which remains, in many ways, based on an old-school individualized connection between buyers and sellers.

The lack of an easy way to buy Bitcoin in 2010 gave a young college dropout named Jed McCaleb an idea. His main venture to that date had been an app named eDonkey2000, a software program designed to make it easy to download music from other people. When that went down in flames (thanks to the copyright law) he had the idea of opening an online trading site for the collectible game *Magic: The Gathering*. That project didn't go well either, but McCaleb held on to the website, named mtgox.com ("Magic: The Gathering Online Exchange"). In 2010, he converted it into a place to buy and sell Bitcoin, and to display current prices. But by 2011 McCaleb had grown sick of running the exchange, so he sold it to Mark Karpelès, a young Frenchman who was living in Japan, the kind of guy who was enthusiastic about writing high-quality backend software.

While Mt. Gox wasn't the only Bitcoin exchange in existence, it took off. It met a latent demand for buying Bitcoin while being somewhat easy to use. By "somewhat," I don't mean actually easy to use—it was still the case that the interface was primitive, and one had to wire real money to a random Japanese bank to buy Bitcoin. There was another weird thing about Mt. Gox: the Bitcoin you bought was held in a "wallet" controlled by the site. In other words, Mt. Gox was both an exchange and a bank at the same time. What could possibly go wrong?

Mt. Gox somehow managed to establish itself as an honest broker. Its presence in Japan, which was not some outlaw nation, seemed to help with legitimacy. Mt. Gox survived hacker attacks in 2011 and was processing some 70 percent of the world's Bitcoin transactions by 2013.[5] At the same time, it also became the holder of much of the world's Bitcoin, as many early buyers of Bitcoin, lacking the time or sophistication to create their own personal "wallet" to store their coins, effectively decided to trust Mt. Gox with their money. Imagine there was one real stock exchange in the world. That it also held on to your money like a bank. And that it was owned and operated by one dude living in Japan with limited life experience. That was Mt. Gox.

Bitcoin may have been decentralized, but Mt. Gox was not. And—surprise!—the centralized design proved unstable. It was constantly targeted by hackers trying to steal Bitcoin. It had regulatory and legal problems, as you might expect from a CEO who knew nothing about finance or law. It didn't help matters that Karpelès, after setting up Mt. Gox, soon lost interest in its day-to-day operations. "He liked the idea of being CEO," a former employee told *Wired* magazine, "but the day-to-day reality bored him."[6] Karpelès may have been, on paper, running the largest crypto exchange in the world, yet in real life he began devoting most of his time to plans for opening a café in the Shibuya neighborhood of Tokyo. Its name would have been "The Bitcoin Cafe," but his criminal prosecution delayed the launch.[*]

One day in 2014, Mt. Gox abruptly closed, taking all of its depositors' money with it (about 850,000 Bitcoin, present value of about $82 billion). Karpelès seemed surprised when he was arrested by the Japanese authorities. In his defense, it turned out that hackers took most of the depositors' money. His misfeasance might have been as much negligence as intentional theft. In any event, that was the effective end of Mt. Gox.

---

[*] In partial fulfillment of his dream, in 2022 a Bitcoin bar named Pubkey opened in New York's Greenwich Village, which has both various Bitcoin memorabilia and a broad selection of hot dogs.

CENTRALIZATION IS HARD TO AVOID

The failure of Mt. Gox proved Bitcoin's original thesis: centralized financial structures are dangerous and unstable. The problem is that no one has really figured out a way to completely avoid centralization and preserve usability. Consequently, the problem afflicting Mt. Gox—the "Youngman problem"—has continued to repeat itself.

Take the story of Faruk Özer, who ran a popular crypto exchange in Turkey named Thodex. All was well until one day in 2021 when he shut it down, took everyone's money, and fled to Albania. Apparently ignorant of the concept of extradition, he was arrested and sent back to Turkey. Prosecutors said he stole about $2 billion from over 300,000 people, and the judge sentenced him to 11,196 years in prison.[7] The story repeated itself in 2022, when Sam Bankman-Fried (also known as SBF), the young operator of the FTX exchange, was found with his hands deep in the piggy bank. Among other things, Bankman-Fried had created his own currency and used client funds to rescue his former girlfriend's investment fund, alongside numerous other activities that managed to consume billions. SBF stood out for his political contributions and celebrity recruitment, as well as his ridiculous philosophical dabblings and pronouncements. ("If you never miss a flight, you're spending too much time in airports.") But in retrospect, he was just a louder variation on the same theme.

The unsolved challenge for Bitcoin decentralization is to maintain a modicum of easy functionality without relying on central exchanges and money storage. There are a number of "decentralized exchanges" in existence (Uniswap is a prominent example), yet they can be more difficult to use and have historically been prone to fraud. It has proven difficult to create something truly accessible to normal people while retaining the original, highly decentralized vision of Bitcoin.

A different answer is to rely on centralized exchanges that are trustworthy because they are heavily government-regulated or have existing reputations in finance. Coinbase—a regulated U.S. firm—has a business model that might be best described as being less shady than the other guys. Fidelity—the brokerage firm founded in 1946—became a limited Bitcoin exchange in the 2020s. Other entities, like BlackRock, began offering Bitcoin ETFs. None of these have stolen anyone's money yet, and none are run by goofballs in their twenties.

But when we speak of BlackRock and Fidelity as central figures in the Bitcoin world, it is evident that something of the original vision has been lost. As Andy Bromberg, CEO of wallet developer Eco, said in 2023, "One day, these Wall Street institutions will own 70% of the Bitcoin in circulation. [. . .] I'm not so sure that is the thing that we were trying to build."[8]

On the other hand, it is possible that no one cares too much about that if the real engine behind it all is less ideological and more material: the lure of easy money. And coupled with the code at the center, this has given Bitcoin something that *The Economist* described as a cockroach-like quality: despite the scandals, Bitcoin is very hard to kill, as the code itself is not tied to any known individual or company. It says something that Bitcoin, despite all the scandals and fraud, keeps marching upward in value, based on the axiom "in code we trust."

Does crypto get any credit for serving to distribute economic power? The backers of crypto projects often speak of serving the unbanked of the world or addressing global inequities. But what the unbanked and small businesses around the world typically lack is capital or access to credit. It is not yet so clear how a digital currency helps with that. Access to a stable currency would indeed help people in countries with untrustworthy currencies store their wealth, which is why the U.S. dollar plays that role in places like Argentina. El Salvador, which uses the U.S. dollar as its currency, adopted Bitcoin as a legal tender in 2021.[9] Yet even in such countries, usage remains limited, because accessing crypto remains a complicated undertaking. The Argentinian peso is as inflationary and unreliable a fiat currency as you can imagine. But while things may change, as it stands you still need to pay for your steaks using pesos.

At this point, crypto hasn't yet made a major dent in the problem of global wealth imbalance. And there seem to be a few missing steps before crypto becomes reasonably accessible and easy to use in a way that benefits the truly poor. "Like any really ambitious project," Altman said of his Worldcoin, "maybe it works out and maybe it doesn't."[10]

The fairest statement about crypto is that while it may not have balanced the global economy, or even been a transfer from rich to poor, it has done the following. It has allowed a class of tech-savvy or risk-accepting people to make significant money. Some of those people are on the younger side. Rebalancing is rebalancing, and that does count for something. But as a solution to the broader problems of economic imbalance and inequality, it is, so far, not yet an answer.

CHAPTER 15

MERE REDISTRIBUTION

If economic imbalances and inequality aren't easily solved by technological solutions or "leaving things to the market," what about good old-fashioned taxation and redistribution? Some might think this is a blindingly obvious answer—if only politicians would come to their senses. In fuller form, it would allow the platforms and other market powers to continue as they are, even hold lasting monopolies, but insist on higher taxes and better redistribution of the proceeds.

There are numerous, important reasons to redistribute money to support the sick, elderly, and unemployed. Social support systems are a foundation of any humane country. But as the only solution to inequality and economic imbalance, redistribution has subtle but serious limits. The main flaw is that an "aggregate wealth now, distribute later" strategy contains the seeds of its own failure. Once people have things, including money or power, they rarely want to give them up. The approach predictably widens imbalances, with the hope that they will be fixed later—but later may never come. Even if successful, the strategy risks the creation of a two-class society with a permanent underclass. These are subtle points that must be explained carefully.

We might well do so by focusing on a key metaphor often used to justify the approach: the national pie.

"DIVIDING THE PIE"

It was in the 1960s that journalists, economists, and politicians began regularly referring to national output as the "national pie"—or sometimes the "national economic pie."[*] The origins of the metaphor are obscure, though it has several things going for it. A pie has always been a symbol of abundance. A pie must be divided before eating, making distribution inevitable. For these reasons the metaphor has a strong appeal to those who want to be both friendly to business and progressive at the same time. As a guide to economic policy, it is fair to say that "grow the pie" has held great influence for much of the last fifty years.

The pie metaphor recommends the following two-step approach to economic policy. First, in step one, you grow the pie as large as possible. Second, you divide the pie among citizens, based on criteria that reflect your political leanings. The pie metaphor leads naturally to a taxation-redistribution approach because it suggests leaving business alone to do its thing (growing the pie) and then, later on, taxing to redistribute the proceeds.

Economic policy is hard and messy, which is why metaphors often end up serving as guides. But as an approach to economic policy, the pie metaphor has been more misleading than you'd think. Even by its own terms, it skips over several key questions, including what goes into making that pie, and, most important, where the proceeds eventually land. For the question of where the money begins (what Jacob Hacker calls "pre-distribution") makes all the difference.

Let's begin with the metaphor itself. There is, of course, no actual national pie or bank account that gets divided up before

---

[*] In the labor context, here's how industrialist Henry Kaiser put it in a 1945 speech: the "wrong way" for unions to achieve a higher standard of living would be "to demand a larger share of the existing national income. A pie that has been baked. The right way is to help make a bigger pie."

being used. Wealth accumulates, instead, in the private accounts of individuals and corporations. There is no necessary step where the pie needs to be or indeed does get divided. Instead, once people make money, they usually don't want to give it up.

Over the last forty years, a more accurate pie metaphor would have pictured pies growing in the backyards of very wealthy individuals and corporations. Take Apple Inc., which decided to pile up cash over the 2010s. By 2021, it had built up a mountain of more than $200 billion in cash, which if stored in bills would have made up a private pie weighing more than 441 million pounds.[1]

The more you allow wealth to accumulate unequally, the more unbalanced the economy becomes—and the harder it becomes to take it away. Economic power consists of the ability to resist redistribution. That's why a policy focused on only growing the pie was also likely, on a systemic basis, to have *prevented* it from being cut in the first place.

TWO-CLASS SOCIETY

Even assuming a government can overcome resistance and redistribute cash away from wealthy individuals and powerful firms, there are reasons to question the long-term appeal of the resulting arrangement. What it threatens to create amounts to a two-class society—a wealthy upper class that supports an impoverished underclass.

Imagine the country that tolerates monopoly power and profit, in order to then hand out money to the poor and other citizens. It divides society into two groups: the owners and managers of the wealth creation engines, and everyone else. The latter group, in an extreme example, becomes employees of, or simply dependent upon, transfer payments. Taken to an extreme, entire regions and countries become part of the dependent class. The arrangement begins to resemble a feudal economy.

Being in the dependent class might not sound so bad if the payments are large enough, but there is an inherent brittleness to the arrangement in more than one respect. For one, it depends on the continued willingness of the ruling class to pay out. That could change—one generation might be charitable, the next generation less so. Second, the monopoly business may become essential to the nation, a sacred cow that needs to be protected at all costs, even if the business is going downhill. Lacking any alternatives, the nation may become like a company town entirely dependent on the local plant and devastated when it leaves.

Finally, if the government seizes enough power to tax and redistribute—perhaps by the rise of a strongman—there's the risk that this more powerful government will become tempted to keep more of the money for itself. Indeed, this is precisely what one sees in many dictatorships that come to power promising to tax the rich and give more of the spoils to the people. After an initial phase of generous handouts, more of the money stays in official hands. A relatively recent example of this outcome comes from the nation of Venezuela, where Hugo Chavez came to power in 1998 promising to take from the rich and give to the poor. Chavez won that election in a landslide and did, at first, hand out money to the needy. But as time went on, he and his state increasingly took more for themselves. Chavez, the servant of the people, managed to make himself a billionaire over his time in office.*

It is also worth asking what it means to live in a class overly dependent on transfer payments. There is, to be sure, a freedom and autonomy anchored in a freedom from want. The strongest case for a system that establishes a kind of trust fund in the sky is that we'd finally feel free not to worry about money, free from the monotony of work, and finally at liberty to do as we please. It is the autonomy enjoyed by a retiree with adequate savings. But that kind of freedom, while of undeniable importance, is only one dimension of economic freedom. There is also a keenly felt sense of autonomy that comes with some control or ownership over one's own means of production, as petty and bourgeois as that may sound.

I return to the position that the two programs are not incom-

---

* Many initially popular dictators, like Robert Mugabe, Muammar Gaddafi, Mao Zedong, and Idi Amin, began by redistributing wealth in public ways and only later began feeding their political rivals to literal or figurative crocodiles.

patible. One can believe in a system of redistribution that provides safeguards and benefits to aid the sick, elderly, and unemployed, while also believing in an economy that distributes economic power widely. In fact, there is a strong reason to believe that the former aids the latter. The mistake is believing or allowing a social safety net to become understood as a substitute for a balanced economy. It is a mistake that has at times infected the left, particularly the American left, which has too often devoted all its energies to fighting for wealth transfer programs while ignoring the deeper questions of economic imbalance.

PART IV

AN ARCHITECTURE OF EQUALITY

One popular vision of the ideal state, particularly among libertarians, is the "night watchman" state, whose main duty is to uphold basic rights against incursion but do little else. That typically means protecting public safety, providing defense against foreign attack, and defending citizens against oppression by the government itself.

But what does the night watchman do about growing private power? Liberty is threatened by private as well as public quarters. A mere night watchman in the economic realm tends, one way or another, to lead to a monopolized economy. That leads to extraction, which leads to anger, which leads to hate—you get the idea. The night watchman does nothing while the country travels the real road to serfdom, in which popular anger about concentrated wealth yields revolution and an authoritarian dictator.

That's why the ideal state, economically speaking, should be understood not as a night watchman but as a gardener of a large and challenging plot. As we've learned previously, the gardener does not seek to grow *in the place of* the plants. She respects that there is a certain genius in, say, a tomato plant or fig tree that is not easily replicated, just as there is a certain genius in complex manufacturing that may be hard for government to replicate well. But if one plant tries to overgrow the whole garden and starve everything else of sun and light, the gardener doesn't throw up her hands and just let nature take its course. The gardener prunes that plant to enable sun and light to reach the other plants. Any successful garden requires structure for healthy growth.

Above all, the ideal economy, much like the ideal garden, is balanced between producers and plots. To extend the metaphor, even a lover of mint (which grows fast) doesn't want mint to take over the whole garden. Yet both gardens and economies move slowly, and the balancing and unbalancing of economies can take many years.

This final part describes the principal components of an architecture of equality in the platform economy. This is not a full program for an economy—a subject of another work. It is, rather, a program for countering the aggregation of economic power in the platforms and meeting the challenge of our times.

CHAPTER 16

PLATFORMS AND THE ARCHITECTURE
OF EQUALITY

A government devoted to the long-term prosperity of its people must have in place structures that are committed to the constant balancing of the economy—the equivalent to checks and balances for political power.

Previous generations who succeeded in creating more equitable societies sought structural balancing through the division of property ownership, the invention of anti-monopoly and related laws, and the organization of labor. But in our times, conceding that platforms are essential, how are they prevented from devouring too much of the economy's proceeds for themselves?

Platforms of all kinds can indeed support and promote a broadly flourishing economy. Yet, as we've learned, they can also become agents of wealth extraction that starve their ecosystems. We have discussed, at some length, the great transformation of the main technology platforms from the 1990s through today. We have seen that they can and have been the promoters and supporters of a broad range of economic activity and can also change and begin to take more—sometimes far too much—for themselves. Let's consider five important ways in which platform power can be managed and balanced.

1. ANTI-MONOPOLY

Platforms are often monopolies and a natural target for anti-monopoly laws. Nonetheless, some argue that platforms must be thought of differently than your average monopolist. Ben Thompson, a popular newsletter author, suggests, for example, that search platforms enjoy a cycle of self-improvement: the more users, the more searches, the more evidence or data upon which to train the engine.[1] That would suggest that it's better to just have one search engine that everyone uses—an efficient monopoly.

The old-fashioned term for this situation is "natural monopoly" and yes, there can be such a thing. Between the city of San Francisco and Marin County to the north, there is more or less only one good place to put a bridge, and so it seems fair to say that the Golden Gate Bridge has a monopoly on vehicular traffic between those two locations.

But the Golden Gate Bridge is an outlier. True natural monopolies in the economy are rare, and markets long imagined to be natural monopolies are not. For many decades it was assumed that the American telephone system would be best run by a single company, Bell. But in fact it was better to have competition, whether from separate long-distance companies or a number of mobile carriers competing for your dollar. Everyone once thought freight trains must be a natural monopoly, but then along came trucks. Even when it comes to bridges, the Golden Gate may be one thing, but between Manhattan and Brooklyn there are multiple sites for bridges and tunnels, and in a sense, the Brooklyn Bridge is in competition with the Manhattan Bridge and various tunnels.

In the tech platform world, declarations of natural monopoly can be premature. eBay, once upon a time, might have been thought to have a monopoly on online auctions, or even "online commerce" based on some simple network economics. But it turned out that there was room for a more handcrafted alternative (Etsy), as well as specialized auction sites, such as for antiques (liveauctioneers.com), and of course the Amazon Marketplace. The potential for viable competitors to Google's search would make declaring it a natural monopoly a terrible idea. The truth is that calling something a natural monopoly can be a dangerously self-fulfilling prophecy.*

The reasons for encouraging competition among tech platforms may sound obvious but should be restated. Any firm gets away with less when facing competitors. They will also find it harder to stop succession and generational change—that is, the new technologies that may come to succeed theirs, which they have an inherent interest in slowing or co-opting.

These all are elementary principles of anti-monopoly law, and the reasons the nation needs a strong and ongoing antitrust enforcement program. The United States came up with these ideas more than a century ago. Yet like any principles, they have a way of being forgotten. During the honeymoon enjoyed by the tech platforms in the 2000s–2010s, they were left to do as they might like, and even allowed to buy their most dangerous competitors (as Facebook did when it bought Instagram) or pay them not to compete (Google, which was paying Apple more than $20 billion a year to stay out of search and to make Google the default on the iPhone).

An anti-monopoly program does not "create" competition. Instead, it takes away the most convenient tools for killing it. It is easier to buy your most dangerous rivals or pay them to stay away than to improve your products. It is easier to threaten resellers or distributors than convince them that your stuff is better. Anti-monopoly programs done right force the dominant firm to fight on the merits. In innovative, technology-centered markets, the very goal of antitrust should be understood as creating the openings for industrial succession, peaceful or otherwise.

Over the 2020s the American anti-monopoly movement staged a comeback. With most of the tech platforms under investigation, we are not speaking of breaking entirely new ground. The so-called antitrust winter—a period of nonenforcement—

---

* There are several technical reasons that natural monopoly is rare. For one thing, the advantages of scale run out at a certain size. The second, demonstrated by the coexistence of eBay and Etsy, is what is called "product differentiation"—slight differences in product or even branding that are enough for consumers to prefer one over another, even in a product that is similar in its underlying nature.

ended with Google's monopoly trial in 2024. But there remains much else that should happen for a platform economy if it is to truly lift all boats.

2. NEUTRALITY RULES—BANS ON BUSINESS DISCRIMINATION

McSorley's Old Ale House in New York's East Village has been a popular place for a long time and has not changed its decor since 1910. In the 1960s its slogan was "Good Ale, Raw Onions, and No Ladies." That changed in 1970, when it was ordered by a federal court to begin serving female customers. Today, when we think of "discrimination," that's the kind of discrimination we have in mind: based on race, gender, or religion. But there's an older type of discrimination ban that was slightly different. It is the ban on arbitrary discrimination by essential businesses against *any* paying customer—a concept that should be an important part of platform oversight.

Consider the story of Ms. de Garton, an Englishwoman with a French name who lived in the fourteenth century. One day she was forcibly ejected from a rural inn for unspecified reasons. It was nighttime, and she was left stranded out in the dark, forced to fend for herself.

Ms. de Garton survived the experience, but she went on to sue the innkeeper. He responded that since the inn was his property he could evict anyone he wanted and whenever he wanted. The case raised an issue that was, at the time, novel. Then, as today, a property owner was entitled to evict anyone from a private home for pretty much any reason. (Have you ever had an annoying dinner guest going on too long about a recent vacation? Anglo-American law allows you to ask that guest to leave, and even summon the sheriff if the guest refuses to go.)

But that's a private home. An inn may be privately owned, but it offers rooms to the public. In the Garton case, an English court decided that the inn was not truly a private concern but a "public calling." It had become a public house (a "pub") by holding itself out to the public as such. And by doing so, it now had duties. And among those duties was a basic one: not to throw paying guests out into the night.

In a similar case in the fifteenth century, a blacksmith refused to shoe a man's horse. The horse later threw the man, and he sued the blacksmith for "failing to render service." Once again, the court held that a blacksmith had a duty to serve all comers— and here is a key principle—without discriminating among them.

Who would have such duties? In England, the judges created an entire class of entities that were labeled "public callings" and, in effect, public platforms. The list was long and included not just innkeepers and blacksmiths but also the owners of bridges, ferries, ports, taxicabs, and many others.

In our times, the great tech platforms should be understood as the public callings of our time and given similar duties. Businesses depend on them; we depend on them; they are, for better or worse, the utilities of contemporary life. And as in those times, there is reason to expect more of them—to impose duties that we do not impose on other businesses.

Most important in this respect are neutrality rules. We have already seen how net neutrality rules were essential to the history of the popular Internet. They bar essential platforms—like broadband—from picking and choosing between customers, and between whose traffic they carry. They are, in that sense, a descendant of the rules that required bridges and ferries to carry everyone.

It isn't hard to see how it could be economically important that a ferry or a bridge, privately owned, serve everyone on equal terms. If the Brooklyn Bridge were to serve drivers carrying only Domino's pizzas, and not others, that would give Domino's an advantage having nothing to do with the quality of the pizza. In that sense, commercial discrimination distorts the competition on the merits that is meant to be the hallmark of a free market system.

Treating similar businesses differently on an essential platform is both bad for the economy and a tool of economic extraction. The arguments in favor, stressing the efficiencies of vertical cooperation, are theoretical and not particularly compelling. During the debates over the neutrality of the Internet in the

2000s, there was never a strong reason given—other than allowing extraction—as to why broadband companies ought to be allowed to treat similar sites differently.

The same logic applies to any public platform, and certainly to any utility platform that has become essential to commerce. Rules prohibiting discrimination, unless justified by matters like fraud prevention, are an obvious foundational rule for a platform economy.

3. COUNTERVAILING POWER REVISITED

We've already encountered the ideas of John Kenneth Galbraith, the small-town Canadian who ended up making his career contributions in the United States. Now mainly remembered as a public intellectual who worked in the Kennedy administration, he also wrote three insightful books on twentieth-century capitalism. The most important for our purposes was *American Capitalism*, which introduced his theory of "countervailing power."

Galbraith, writing in the early 1950s, believed that the U.S. economy would be dominated for some time by a small number of large corporations—like General Motors and U.S. Steel. To his credit, Galbraith recognized that this would yield serious danger: an extraordinary concentration of economic power in a small number of firms, effectively immune from competitive forces, that could gain the power of "exploitation"—raise prices, drive down wages, and influence politics, among other toxic effects.

Having worked with Keynes, Galbraith did not believe that "perfect competition" would solve this problem. He believed instead that the key was "countervailing power"—which is to say, the power not of those who compete but of those who bargain with a giant. He argued that countervailing power could prevent economic exploitation. Unfortunately, Galbraith presumed that such countervailing power could be expected to arise automatically (he was wrong). But the concept is of such importance that we need to examine it more carefully.

Let's stop and explain this point more clearly. The power of a giant firm like General Motors of the 1950s was constrained not just by its direct competitors (like Ford) but also by its suppliers. In the case of GM, it needs steel, and it also needs workers to build the cars. Hence, the steel manufacturers and the employees (if organized) can operate as a constraint on GM and its ability to raise prices, lower wages, or do other similar things.

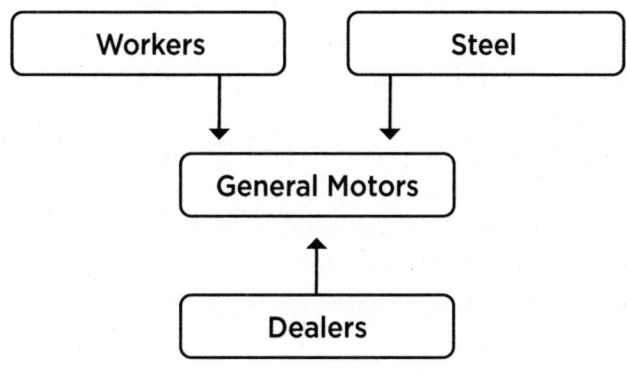

FIG 1. COUNTERVAILING POWER

Unfortunately, having made clear this insight, Galbraith proceeded to make a terrible error, as we discussed above. After identifying the importance of countervailing power, he proceeded to imagine it was a self-generating force that automatically negated accumulated private power. "As a common rule," he wrote, "we can rely on countervailing power to appear as a curb on economic power."

Even if Galbraith was wrong to consider his countervailing power a self-generating force, he was not wrong to see that it could be an important ingredient in the restraint of economic power. And in any program designed to restrain the ascendant power of the tech platforms, the countervailing power of those they deal with is an essential element.

It follows that the law should attempt to empower those in a position to restrain platform power. Who they are depends on the platform in question, but here are some of the candidates:

OWNERS OF VALUABLE INFORMATION. Some platforms depend on valuable content or information—news being the most obvious example. Collectively, the world's newspapers, artists, and authors carry enough economic weight to seriously limit the tech platforms. To take just one example, artificial intelligence language models cannot train and cannot exist without authored text, and much of the most valuable text is copyrighted. If the owners of copyright are able to effectively police access to their works, they can function as a countervailing power.

WORKERS. Workers are an obvious constraint on the power of any business or frankly any institution. There is no company without its workers, whether they are full-time salaried, part-time, or independent contractors. Yet an individual worker, especially one desperate for a job, is entirely outmatched against a large employer. That first became evident during the Industrial Revolution. The fact that legislation in England passed in 1847 limiting children to a ten-hour workday gives a sense of the situation.[2] Giant employers became more distant from their workers and began to see their labor as a commodity, something to extract maximum value from at minimum cost, not unlike a farm animal or a slave.

The economic case for unions is quite straightforward. It creates a competitive balance of countervailing powers. In theory, it might even replicate the conditions of "perfect competition"—if the market power of the union and the employer are evenly matched. The logic helps explain why, by the mid-1950s, in the United States, about one-third of private-sector workers were unionized.[3] That year was also, whether by coincidence or not, the year that income inequality was at its lowest in the United States.[4]

Since then, something has gone terribly wrong for workers. Real wages for the middle and lower classes stagnated from the 1970s through 2020 or so.[5] Both income and wealth inequality reached extraordinary and unprecedented levels. The share of the economy's proceeds that went to labor as opposed to capital entered a steady decline from the 1970s onward.[6]

Membership in unions, as noted earlier, are way down, from 34 percent to about 7 percent of the private workforce.[7] Entire new industries, such as tech, including the more industrial parts, haven't unionized in significant ways. And the consolidation of many industries has greatly reduced competition for employees in many sectors. One example is in the hospital sector, where competition for workers and salaries goes down after consolidation into giant super-hospitals.[8]

In the 1980s, a different theory of worker protection emerged that cast unions as unnecessary because employers needed to treat workers well as a matter of enlightened self-interest. Here's Denny Strigl, former Verizon executive and leadership consultant, writing in 2012: "In the modern business world, unions are obsolete. Workers no longer need a union to be treated fairly by their employers and most public sector employers today provide excellent wages and benefits."[9] Tim Sackett, an HR consultant, put it this way: "Employers can't afford to treat employees badly."[10]

These arguments resonate with a classic American belief: that everyone is above average. Hence, everyone will do better than everyone else when negotiating for salary, benefits, and so on. If each of us is special, then we will each be fairly treated by an employer, just as we were treated as special by our parents.

While I would not entirely discount the power of human beneficence, the theory ignores the pressure that most corporate management faces in order to reduce costs and boost profitability. The single largest cost, for most firms, is employee salaries and benefits. When managerial performance is measured by cost reduction, it tends to overwhelm whatever generous sentiments management may hold in their hearts. They don't want to be fired either.

Over the twenty-first century, exploitative employment practices have spread to higher-ranking employees. Professionals, management, and even executives have come to suffer from abysmal working conditions. For this class, the pay is obviously far better. But in many professional jobs, overwork and stress are the norm, with pressure to do more in less time. Individual veterinarians, nurses, and doctors face pressure to spend less time with patients. Lawyering has become such a treadmill that associates regularly compare their firms to sweatshops. Professionals often work hours that resemble those of nineteenth-century steelwork-ers, at significant costs to their physical and mental health. Our various labor-saving technologies designed to make work more efficient have not managed to make for less work.

The theory of countervailing power points to organized labor as the force that would make work better and better paid. That said, today's unions are hardly perfect. Like any large and aged institution, they show distinct signs of suffering from stag-nation and the curse of bigness. Born to face giant manufactur-ing firms like GM and Ford, unions can, unfortunately, resemble them. That's what makes the enlargement and improvement of employee representation an important project. "There is no hope for American democracy," said Justice Louis Brandeis, "unless the American working man is permitted to combine, and, through combination and collective bargaining, secure for him-self the rights of industrial liberty."[11]

4. UTILITY RULES AND CAPS

Warren Buffett, the famed investor, has said more than once that his ideal investment looks like a toll bridge.[12] Whatever else hap-pens, everyone needs the bridge, and it can, in theory, set any price it likes. If San Francisco's Golden Gate Bridge were pri-vately operated and unregulated, it would be, as Buffett surmised, a fairly risk-free license to print money.

There are examples of such lucrative private bridges in Amer-ican history. The Charles River Bridge, which connects Boston to Charlestown, was built in 1786 and was entirely owned by private shareholders.[13] According to its owners, it cost $51,000 to build. By the 1800s, that investment had earned out, and by 1827, the bridge was a figurative cash cow—all revenue and few costs, earning an estimated income of $30,000 per year.[14] That was actually enough to make it one of the more profitable busi-nesses in the United States. As one contemporary put it, "The profits of the bridge have been great beyond the example of any similar institution in this country."

The monopoly toll bridge is certainly good for investors, but bad for everyone else, because it operates as a tax on the rest of the economy. It is a clear example of how an entity meant to support economic activity can become an albatross. When it was built, the Charles River Bridge was surely a boon to economic activity in the Boston area. But by the 1820s, after being fully paid out, the Charles River Bridge was just an extraction machine. The point—if it is not already obvious—is that then and now, platforms are the essential infrastructure of commerce in our time.

The major tech platforms can and have become Charles River Bridges: agents of excessive extraction that have already paid off investors and begun operating like a private tax. We've seen that Amazon takes so much from its businesses that they remain constantly squeezed. Google has ensured much of the advertising revenue in the online world flows in its direction. And so on.

One answer is to build alternatives. In the case of the actual Charles River Bridge, the legislature, receptive to public anger, built another bridge over the same span, financed by tolls that went to zero after six years. In other words, the new bridge became free to use after some time, providing the same function without being a drain on the rest of the economy.

But when all else fails, the answer—admittedly a last resort—is to declare an essential platform to be a utility and place a hard cap on what the platform can take from the rest of the economy. This must be done carefully and when the facts have become clear. The practice is most clearly established for electricity and other energy providers, which few can do without. After all, Americans already spend nearly $230 billion per year on residential electricity and gas; and that's with limits on monopoly pricing.[15]

Caps for utility services apply to other, newer industries too. As we shall see, Europe and its treatment of credit and debit cards provides a model. Credit and debit cards hide the amount they charge from consumers, by charging it to the retailer. American Express, for example, claims about 3 percent of the purchase price for using its card.[16] So, if you're buying a $100 item, the credit card takes $3, but you don't see it; it is instead swallowed by the retailer, who makes prices higher to compensate. It doesn't, of course, actually cost American Express anything close to $3 to process the transaction, which explains the $8.4 billion of profit it earned in 2023. In this sense, credit cards truly impose a hidden tax on much of the economy—Americans spent some $135.75 billion in fees in 2023 alone.[17]

In the United States, the hope has been that competition and the free market might keep such fees in check. But since consumers don't actually see the prices charged—as they are hidden away—competition has not worked well. Fees have instead steadily increased, particularly since 2020. Innovations like the Discover card, which attempts to refund the fees in whole or in part, have only been partially successful in arresting a general and inflationary rise in fees.

Europe takes a more straightforward approach: a simple cap on what credit cards can add to the purchase. The cap is 0.3 percent.[18] If you're spending $100 in Europe, the credit card can take no more than 30 cents from that transaction, more than covering its costs but eliminating hidden fees as a major profit source.

Utility rate settings can go wrong—for example, they might discourage investment. They must be used wisely, especially in newer markets where business models may not have settled. But in situations like the toll bridge and the credit card—where so-called market remedies have failed—caps can put a stop to evident wealth extraction that provides no social benefit.

5. QUARANTINES AND "LINE OF BUSINESS" RESTRICTIONS

Given the extraordinary power of the tech platforms, sometimes the best answer is to impose strict limits on what lines of business the firm may operate in. These are known as quarantines, or "line of business" restrictions. The idea is to keep the monopoly power separate from other areas of business so that they may thrive.

Such separations are more common than you might realize. Retail stores, for example, are prohibited from operating banks, which is why Walmart doesn't have its own banking operation. In the history of technological development, there are examples where such quarantines have effectively driven innovation and growth. From the 1950s through the mid-1980s, AT&T, the great telephone monopolist, was explicitly barred by court decree from computing and semiconductors, leaving the field open to the growth of an independent industry.

What could that mean for the platform economy? It could be used in manners small and large. In the case of our quintessential commerce platform, the Amazon Marketplace, this would suggest banning Amazon from selling its own goods in competition with its dependent businesses. Such product lines are just a fraction of Amazon's revenue, and the product managers of such units have shown their willingness to take unfair advantages. Some might mourn the loss of the Amazon battery, though of course, the underlying firm that makes the battery could still sell it ("the battery formerly known as the Amazon battery"). The point is that the revenue earned from those brands, while insignificant to Amazon, is a serious drag on independent business and wealth creation by those other than the platform owner. It is one easy and obvious thing to fix.

A larger separation might seek to keep a distance between today's tech platforms and ownership of the main technologies of artificial intelligence. There is a strong case for restraining the existing platforms from using their monopolistic power to dominate the artificial intelligence markets. We should want the AI sector to make a real challenge to the monopolistic platforms born in the 2000s or earlier. The simplest version of this would bar the existing tech platforms from buying or controlling new AI platforms such as OpenAI and others.

The most important long-term constraint on today's platforms will be the rise of challengers who are independent from them. And that might only happen if there is room to grow—the prevention of domination of AI by Microsoft, Google, and similar firms.

There is no silver bullet remedy to counter the dangers of excessive wealth extraction by the platforms. It is also pointless to suggest that we can somehow do without tech platforms or some equivalent. What history suggests is that there have always been and will always be spaces, physical or otherwise, essential to commerce and human transactions. Instead, the point is to create structures with the goal of restraining monopoly and aiding the balancing of economic powers—in the interests of a broader prosperity.

EPILOGUE

Every moment is a turning point, but some are more significant than others. Over the early twenty-first century it seemed apparent that humanity was being squeezed to the breaking point. Anger and resentment are dominant public emotions, yielding a renewed worship of power. The anger may be directed superficially at scapegoats, but its origins can be traced to economic causes. Too many people feel the system is broken and does not work for them. And as the evolution of platforms has shown, our online technologies carry their own power and can evolve to serve nonhuman ends. At its worst, artificial intelligence could well become an accomplice to the corporation in the marginalization and commodification of humanity.

But if this diagnosis is not uplifting, there is still reason to have hope for our technological future. That doesn't mean buying into the dogmatic, quasi-religious form of tech optimism that has gripped parts of Silicon Valley, which takes any critique of the tech industry as a form of heresy. What we're in need of is something more like guarded, rule-driven optimism of earlier figures like science fiction author Isaac Asimov.

Asimov is famous for writing about artificially intelligent

robots in the 1950s and 1960s at the dawn of computing. As a young author he was determined to avoid the "Frankenstein" mold in which the machine always turns on its creator. Instead he forecast a future where advanced computing could greatly benefit humanity but not without economic and social risks. He took the key challenge as getting the rules right: in particular, he outlined the "three laws of robotics" to which all robots were bound. (The most important was the first, which was a duty to never harm a human, or through inaction, allow a human to come to harm.) This is a perspective that suggests that there is nothing inherently good or evil about the technologies of our future. It is rather a duty for both the private and public sectors to create products that actually serve humanity.

If we have gone astray, we can also take some solace in our capacity to repair and restore. By this point, with its classic 1970s design, the Internet is a mature and tested infrastructure upon which much has been built. The platform itself is an ancient invention, and it has stood the test of time as a foundation of human thriving. When the platform plays a supportive role, when it serves to enable and empower others, it is among the greatest agents of economic liberation ever devised. The problem, as we've shown over the course of this book, is that our tech platforms have outgrown their boundaries. You might say that they suffer from main character syndrome. They forget that their role is to host and support the activities of others, not to be the show themselves.

It is not too late to restore the early promise of the Internet economy as a common square for commerce and an agent of economic uplift for all. We can take hope from the story of city squares and marketplaces like New York's Union Square, La Boqueria Market in Barcelona, and London's Covent Garden. Each of these was a thriving hub of activity in the nineteenth century linked to nearby shopping streets in great cities. Over the twentieth century each declined and became derelict thanks to developments like the rise of the car, the decline of cities, and the rise of the drug trade. Yet over the last forty years, each of these city markets and squares—thanks to determined and deliberate effort—has been revitalized. These city squares can be too crowded and too touristy. But they are vibrant and bustling, as are the areas surrounding them. They show the lasting qualities of ancient infrastructure like the city square and city street, and their capacity to outlast fads, fashions, and political changes.

The recovery of a broadly prosperous economy will not be accomplished overnight. But as difficult as it may be to believe, there have been periods in which the economy really did work for most of the population. The key is recovering a healthy skepticism of accumulated economic power, which goes hand in hand with distrusting unaccountable power no matter what form it takes. The last few decades have shown the folly in blindly relying on the beneficence of institutions never designed to promote humanity's best interests. But we can do better, and should do better, to achieve a future of broad and lasting prosperity for everyone.

ACKNOWLEDGMENTS

My thanks to Tina Bennett, who is so good at her job and saw this project through many stages (including a long pause for government service). To Quynh Do for editing and shepherding, and the Knopf team more generally for believing in the project and publishing the entire trilogy. Thanks to the staff of Stillwater Coffee, especially Will, who tolerated long sits. My thanks to my team of research assistants, especially Ana Lentini, Michael Swerdlow, Nora Franco, and Katie Mimini, and my assistant, Marta Torelli. Columbia faculty generously provided feedback on drafts, and thanks also for readings by Leon Wieseltier, Scott Hemphill, Gill Wu, and Kate.

I am deeply grateful to my wife, Kate, whose encouragement and support meant a great deal throughout this project. And to my daughters, Sierra and Essie, "without whose never-failing sympathy and encouragement this book would have been finished in half the time."

NOTES

INTRODUCTION

1. Apple, "Crush! | iPad Pro | Apple," YouTube, May 7, 2024, 1:08, https://www.youtube.com/watch?v=ntjkwIXWtrc.
2. Julian Sanction, "Apple's 'Soul-Crushing' New Ad: Who Thought This Was a Good Idea?," *Hollywood Reporter*, May 8, 2024, https://www.hollywoodreporter.com/business/business-news/apple-soul-crushing-new-ipad-ad-dystopian-1235893898/.
3. Bobby Allyn, "Scarlett Johansson Says She Is 'Shocked, Angered' over New ChatGPT Voice," NPR, May 20, 2024, https://www.npr.org/2024/05/20/1252495087/openai-pulls-ai-voice-that-was-compared-to-scarlett-johansson-in-the-movie-her.
4. James Colgan, "Meet Digital Jack Nicklaus, Golf Legend's Metaverse 'Twin' Featured on BBC," *Golf*, December 13, 2022, https://golf.com/lifestyle/digital-jack-nicklaus-metaverse-avatar/.
5. Steven Levy, "What the Techno-Billionaire Missed About Techno-Optimism," *Wired*, October 28, 2023, https://www.wired.com/story/plaintext-marc-andreessen-techno-billionaire-wrong-techno-optimism/.
6. "Advancing Decentralization," *Worldcoin Blog*, Dec. 6, 2023, https://worldcoin.org/blog/foundational-topics/advancing-decentralization.
7. Sam Altman, "The Intelligence Age," September 23, 2024, https://ia.samaltman.com/.
8. Nate Silver, *On the Edge* (New York: Penguin Press, 2024).
9. Jim Sindreu, "In Sports, American Socialism Is Beating European Capitalism," *Wall Street Journal*, October 18, 2024, https://www.wsj.com/sports

/soccer/in-sports-american-socialism-is-beating-european-capitalism
-e6ca0e6a.

10. Alexis de Tocqueville, *Democracy in America*, vol. 2 (New York: Vintage
Books, 1990).

PART I: UNDERSTANDING PLATFORM POWER

1. Jeff Jarvis, *What Would Google Do?* (New York: Harper Business, 2009).
2. Jarvis, *What Would Google Do?*
3. Yochai Benkler, *The Wealth of Networks: How Social Production Transforms Markets and Freedom* (New Haven, CT: Yale University Press, 2006).

1. THE GENIUS OF THE ANCIENT CITY SQUARE

1. *Encyclopaedia Britannica*, s.v. "agora," accessed June 7, 2024, https://www
.britannica.com/topic/agora.
2. Jean-Charles Rochet and Jean Tirole, "Platform Competition in Two-Sided Markets," *Journal of the European Academic Association* 1, no. 4 (2003).
3. George A. Akerlof, "The Market for 'Lemons': Quality Uncertainty and the Market Mechanism," *Quarterly Journal of Economics* 84, no. 3 (1970).
4. Mark Overton, *Agricultural Revolution in England: The Transformation of the Agrarian Economy 1500–1850* (Cambridge: Cambridge University Press, 1996).

2. PLATFORMIZATION

1. David Leonhardt, "John Tukey, 85, Statistician; Coined the Word 'Software,'" *New York Times*, July 28, 2000, https://www.nytimes.com/2000/07
/28/us/john-tukey-85-statistician-coined-the-word-software.html.
2. John Tukey, "The Teaching of Concrete Mathematics," *American Mathematical Monthly* 65, no. 1 (1958).
3. "Data Tools," U.S. Bureau of Economic Analysis, accessed October 1, 2024, https://www.bea.gov/tools.
4. "IBM / 360," *Computer History Museum*, accessed October 1, 2024, https://
www.computerhistory.org/revolution/mainframe-computers/7/161#:~:
text=IBM's%20revenue%20in%201962%20was,new%20peripherals%20
%E2%80%94%20with%20great%20fanfare.
5. "Computers: Do-All Thinkmachine," *Time*, April 17, 1964, https://time
.com/archive/6813564/computers-do-all-thinkmachine/.
6. Albert H. Walker, *History of the Sherman Law of the United States of America* (New York: Baker, Voorhis, 1910).
7. Thurman Arnold, address to the American Bar Association, July 10, 1939.
8. 96 Cong. Rec. 16,452 (1950).
9. "Watson Jr. Memo About CDC 6600," *Computer History Museum*, accessed October 1, 2024, https://www.computerhistory.org/revolution
/supercomputers/10/33/62.

10. Robert Bork, "Neutral Principles and Some First Amendment Problems," *Yale Law Journal* 47, no. 1 (1971).
11. Tim Wu, "Tech Dominance and the Policeman at the Elbow," in *After the Digital Tornado: Networks, Algorithms, Humanity*, ed. Kevin Werbach (Cambridge: Cambridge University Press, 2020).
12. Stanley Gibson, "Software Industry Born with IBM's Unbundling," *Computerworld*, June 19, 1989.
13. Gibson, "Software Industry Born with IBM's Unbundling."
14. Marie Anchordoguy, *Computers, Inc: Japan's Challenge to IBM* (Cambridge, MA: Harvard University Asia Center, 1989).
15. Martin Campbell-Kelly, *From Airline Reservations to Sonic the Hedgehog: A History of the Software Industry* (Cambridge, MA: MIT Press, 2003).
16. Tom Mahoney, *The Story of George Romney: Builder, Salesman, Crusader* (New York: Harper & Brothers, 1960).
17. "Licklider Describes the 'Intergalactic Computer Network,'" *History of Information*, accessed October 5, 2024, https://www.historyofinformation.com/detail.php?entryid=1029.
18. Katie Hafner and Matthew Lyon, *Where Wizards Stay Up Late: The Origins of the Internet* (New York: Touchstone, 1996).
19. Hafner and Lyon, *Where Wizards Stay Up Late: The Origins of the Internet.*
20. Hafner and Lyon, *Where Wizards Stay Up Late: The Origins of the Internet.*

3. THE GOLDEN AGE OF TECH OPTIMISM

1. David A. Kaplan, *The Silicon Boys: And Their Valley of Dreams* (New York: William Morrow, 1999).
2. Clay Shirky, *Here Comes Everybody: The Power of Organizing Without Organizations* (New York: Penguin, 2008).
3. Glenn Reynolds, *An Army of Davids: How Markets and Technology Empower Ordinary People to Beat Big Media, Big Government, and Other Goliaths* (Nashville: Thomas Nelson, 2006).
4. Yochai Benkler, "Coase's Penguin, or, Linux and "The Nature of the Firm," *Yale Law Journal* 112, no. 3 (2002).
5. As mentioned in the preamble to Part I.
6. Peter Thiel and Blake Masters, *Zero to One: Notes on Startups, or How to Build the Future* (New York: Crown Business, 2014).
7. Jeff Jarvis, *What Would Google Do?* (New York: Collins Business, 2009).
8. Thiel and Masters, *Zero to One: Notes on Startups, or How to Build the Future.*
9. "Founders' IPO Letter," *Alphabet Investor Relations*, accessed October 6, 2024, https://abc.xyz.
10. Tim Wu, *The Attention Merchants* (New York: Penguin Random House, 2016).
11. Dominic Rushe, "Google Buys Waze Map App for $1.3bn," *The Guardian*, June 11, 2013, https://www.theguardian.com/technology/2013/jun/11/google-buys-waze-maps-billion.

4. FROM ENABLEMENT TO EXTRACTION—
THE STORY OF THE AMAZON MARKETPLACE

1. Jeff Jarvis, *What Would Google Do?* (New York: Collins Business, 2009).
2. "World's Largest Bookseller Opens on the Web," *Amazon Press Center*, October 4, 1995, https://press.aboutamazon.com.
3. Hal R. Varian, "Reading Between the Lines of Used Book Sales," *New York Times*, July 28, 2005, https://www.nytimes.com/2005/07/28/technology /reading-between-the-lines-of-used-book-sales.html.
4. "Amazon Marketplace Statistics," *Capital One Shopping Research*, October 29, 2024, https://capitaloneshopping.com/research/amazon-marketplace -statistics/.
5. "Amazon Launches New Services to Help Small and Medium-Sized Businesses Enhance Their Customer Offerings by Accessing Amazon's Order Fulfillment, Customer Service, and Website Functionality," *Amazon Press Center*, September 19, 2006, https://press.aboutamazon.com /2006/9/amazon-launches-new-services-to-help-small-and-medium-sized -businesses-enhance-their-customer-offerings-by-accessing-amazons -order-fulfillment-customer-service-and-website-functionality.
6. Rupert Neate, "Amazon Reports $89bn in Sales Last Year as Shares Jump 11% After Hours," *The Guardian*, January 29, 2015, https://www .theguardian.com/technology/2015/jan/29/amazon-reports-89b-in-sales -2014.
7. "Ebay Cuts 2014 Revenue Forecast, Shares Tumble," Reuters, October 15, 2014, https://www.reuters.com/article/business/ebay-cuts-2014-revenue -forecast-shares-tumble-idUSL2N0SA2XS/.
8. Stacy Mitchell, "Amazon's Monopoly Tollbooth in 2023," Institute for Local Self-Reliance, September 21, 2023, https://ilsr.org/articles/amazonmonopoly tollbooth-2023/.
9. Mitchell, "Amazon's Monopoly Tollbooth in 2023."
10. Dara Kerr, "Amazon Sellers Say They Made a Good Living—Until Amazon Figured It Out," NPR, October 11, 2023, https://www.npr.org/2023 /10/11/1204264632/amazon-sellers-prices-monopoly-lawsuit.
11. Sarah Mae Tejares, "Distil Union Co-Founders Nate Justiss and Lindsay Windham on Tech Times Exclusives #55," *Tech Times*, September 27, 2022, https://www.techtimes.com/articles/281116/20220927/distil-union-co -founders-nate-justiss-lindsay-windham-tech-times.htm.
12. Mitchell, "Amazon's Monopoly Tollbooth in 2023."
13. Eugene Kim, "Amazon's Prime Membership Program Stopped Growing in the US for the First Time Ever, According to New Estimates," *Business Insider*, January 18, 2023, https://www.businessinsider.com/amazon -shopping-prime-membership-us-stopped-growing-first-time-ever-2023-1.
14. "Amazon FBA: Fulfillment Services for Your Ecommerce Business," Fulfillment by Amazon, accessed October 6, 2024, https://sell.amazon.com.
15. Tim Peterson, "Amazon's Ad Revenue Crossed $609 Million in 2012," *AdAge*, June 4, 2013, https://adage.com/article/digital/amazon-s-ad-revenue -crossed-609-million-2012/241834.
16. Garett Sloane, "Amazon Makes Major Leap in Ad Industry with $10 Billion

Year," *AdAge*, January 31, 2019, https://adage.com/article/digital/amazon
-makes-quick-work-ad-industry-10-billion-year/316468.

17. Julia Faria, "Advertising Revenue of Amazon Worldwide from 2019 to
2023," Statista, February 29, 2024, https://www.statista.com/statistics
/259814/amazons-worldwide-advertising-revenue-development/.

18. J. G. Navarro, "Newspaper Advertising Spending Worldwide from 2019 to
2023," Statista, April 29, 2024, https://www.statista.com/statistics/238143
/global-newspapers-advertising-revenue/.

19. Benedict Evans, "Retail, Search and Amazon's $40bn 'Advertising' Busi-
ness," *Benedict Evans*, March 6, 2023, https://www.ben-evans.com
/benedictevans/2023/3/6/ways-to-think-about-amazon-advertising.

20. Mitchell, "Amazon's Monopoly Tollbooth in 2023."

21. Juozas Kaziukėnas, "Amazon Takes a 50% Cut of Sellers' Revenue,"
Marketplace Pulse, February 13, 2023, https://www.marketplacepulse.com
/articles/amazon-takes-a-50-cut-of-sellers-revenue.

22. Kaziukėnas, "Amazon Takes a 50% Cut of Sellers' Revenue."

23. Ed Ponsi, "Walmart's Online and Well-Heeled Appeal," *TheStreet Pro*,
May 17, 2024, https://pro.thestreet.com/trade-ideas/walmarts-online-and
-well-heeled-appeal.

24. Mitchell, "Amazon's Monopoly Tollbooth in 2023."

25. Annie Palmer, "Amazon Accused of Copying Camera Gear Maker's Top-
Selling Item," *CNBC*, March 4, 2021, https://www.cnbc.com/2021/03/04
/amazon-accused-of-copying-camera-gearmaker-peak-designs-top-selling
-item-.html.

26. Dana Mattioli, "Amazon Scooped Up Data from Its Own Sellers to Launch
Competing Products," *Wall Street Journal*, April 23, 2020, https://www.wsj
.com/articles/amazon-scooped-up-data-from-its-own-sellers-to-launch
-competing-products-11587650015.

27. Mattioli, "Amazon Scooped Up Data from Its Own Sellers to Launch
Competing Products."

28. Mitchell, "Amazon's Monopoly Tollbooth in 2023."

29. Wu_Kang, "If we could make similar sales elsewhere, we would, but we
can't. Every 'improvement' Amazon makes is to extract as much revenue
from your sales as possible," Reddit, accessed November 22, 2024, https://
www.reddit.com/r/FulfillmentByAmazon/comments/13n2yod/any_seller
_actually_like_selling_on_amazon/.

5. SCALE AS A WEAPON

1. Pete Wells, "As Not Seen on TV," *New York Times*, November 13, 2012,
https://www.nytimes.com/2012/11/14/dining/reviews/restaurant-review
-guys-american-kitchen-bar-in-times-square.html.

2. Tim Sullivan, "Blitzscaling," *Harvard Business Review*, April 2016, https://
hbr.org/2016/04/blitzscaling?ref=refind.

3. Sullivan, "Blitzscaling."

4. Peter Thiel and Blake Masters, *Zero to One: Notes on Startups, or How to
Build the Future* (New York: Crown Business, 2014).

5. T. Boone Pickens, *Boone* (Boston: Houghton Mifflin, 1987).
6. Sullivan, "Blitzscaling."
7. Reid Hoffman and Chris Yeh, *Blitzscaling: The Lightning-Fast Path to Building Massively Valuable Companies* (New York: Currency, 2018).
8. Sullivan, "Blitzscaling."
9. Friedrich Wilhelm Nietzsche, *Beyond Good and Evil: Prelude to a Philosophy of the Future*, trans. R. J. Hollingdale (New York: Penguin, 2003).
10. Thiel and Masters, *Zero to One: Notes on Startups, or How to Build the Future*.
11. Mike Isaac, "Instagram's User Base Explodes, Surpasses 40 Million," *Wired*, April 13, 2012, https://www.wired.com/2012/04/instagram-40-million-users/.
12. Associated Press, "Google Loses Massive Antitrust Case over Its Search Dominance," NPR, August 5, 2024, https://www.npr.org/2024/08/05/nx -s1-5064624/google-justice-department-antitrust-search.
13. Tim Wu and Stuart A. Thompson, "The Roots of Big Tech Run Disturbingly Deep," *New York Times*, June 7, 2019, https://www.nytimes.com /interactive/2019/06/07/opinion/google-facebook-mergers-acquisitions -antitrust.html.
14. Noam Bardin, "Why Did I Leave Google Or, Why Did I Stay So Long?" LinkedIn, August 14, 2021, https://www.linkedin.com/pulse/why-did-i -leave-google-stay-so-long-noam-bardin/.
15. Bardin, "Why Did I Leave Google Or, Why Did I Stay So Long?"

6. THE GREAT HARVEST

1. Tim Wu, "Content and Its Discontents," *New York Times*, July 18, 2014, https://www.nytimes.com/2014/07/20/books/review/the-peoples-platform -by-astra-taylor.html.
2. Cory Doctorow, "'Enshittification' Is Coming for Absolutely Everything," *Financial Times*, February 7, 2024, https://www.ft.com/content/6fb1602d -a08b-4a8c-bac0-047b7d64aba5.
3. Jaron Lanier, *Who Owns the Future?* (New York: Simon & Schuster, 2013).
4. Amanda Parsons and Salomé Viljoen, "Valuing Social Data," *Columbia Law Review* 124, no. 4 (2023).
5. Chavie Lieber, "How and Why Do Influencers Make So Much Money? The Head of an Influencer Agency Explains," *Vox*, November 18, 2018, https://www.vox.com/the-goods/2018/11/28/18116875/influencer -marketing-social-media-engagement-instagram-youtube.
6. Mattie Kahn, "Is There Life After Influencing?," *New York Times*, April 11, 2023.
7. Kahn, "Is There Life After Influencing?"
8. John Riley, "Young Creators Are Burning Out and Breaking Down," *Here-Now Help*, September 14, 2023.
9. Kahn, "Is There Life After Influencing?"
10. Sam Gutelle, "In New Video, Elle Mills Talks Mental Health, a Break from Social Media, and Being 'Burnt Out at 19,'" *Tubefilter*, May 21, 2018, https://www.tubefilter.com/2018/05/21/elle-mills-mental-health/.
11. Elle Mills, "Youtube Gave Me Everything. Then I Grew Up," *New York*

Times, February 5, 2023, https://www.nytimes.com/2023/02/05/opinion
/elle-mills-youtube-quit.html.

PART II: THE BUSINESS OF HERDING

1. Krystal Hur, "Jim Cramer Says His Group of FANG Tech Companies
   Have Lost Their Magic," *CNBC*, January 30, 2023, https://www.cnbc.com
   /2023/01/30/jim-cramer-says-his-group-of-fang-tech-companies-have
   -lost-their-magic.html.
2. Adam Hayes, "FAAMG Stocks: Acronym for American Tech Stocks,"
   Investopedia, September 23, 2022.

7. A LONG SLOW BET ON LAZINESS

1. "The Border (1982)," *The Movie Database*, accessed on December 3, 2024.
2. Jennifer Maas, "Amazon Closes $8.5 Billion Acquisition of MGM," *Variety*,
   March 17, 2022, https://variety.com/2022/tv/news/amazon-mgm-merger
   -close-1235207852/.
3. Lillian Rizzo, "NFL 'Sunday Ticket' Goes to YouTube in Seven-Year,
   $2 Billion Annual Deal," *CNBC*, December 22, 2022, https://www.cnbc
   .com/2022/12/22/nfl-sunday-ticket-youtube-tv.html; Josh Sim, "Report:
   Amazon and Google Leading Race for NFL's Sunday Ticket," *Sports Pro
   Media*, December 19, 2022, https://www.sportspro.com/news/nfl-sunday
   -ticket-amazon-google-apple-drop-out-disney/.
4. Tim Wu, *The Curse of Bigness* (Columbia Global Reports, 2018).
5. Alina Selyukh, "Amazon Raises Price of Annual Prime Membership
   to $139," NPR, February 3, 2022, https://www.npr.org/2022/02/03
   /1077088524/amazon-raises-price-of-annual-prime-membership-to-139.
6. "Facebook User & Growth Statistics," *Backlinko*, September 4, 2024,
   https://backlinko.com/facebook-users; "Instagram Statistics: Key Demo-
   graphic and User Numbers," *Backlinko*, November 21, 2024, https://
   backlinko.com/instagram-users.
7. Tim Berners-Lee, *Weaving the Web: The Original Design and Ultimate Destiny of the World Wide Web by Its Inventor* (San Francisco: Harper, 1999).
8. Including my own *Attention Merchants*. The induction of (nonphysical)
   addiction by the social media sites is well covered in *Irresistible: The Rise
   of Addictive Technology and the Business of Keeping Us Hooked* by Adam Alter,
   and early on, Nicholas Carr's *The Shallows: What the Internet Is Doing to Our
   Brains*.
9. "Couchlock," *Urban Dictionary*, accessed November 22, 2024.
10. Kate Conger and Lauren Hirsch, "Elon Musk Completes $44 Billion Deal
    to Own Twitter," *New York Times*, October 27, 2022, https://www.nytimes
    .com/2022/10/27/technology/elon-musk-twitter-deal-complete.html.
11. Deepak Upadhyay, "Back Elon Musk Shares Update on X 'Everything
    App,'" *mint*, March 25, 2024.

8. BIG DATA, KNOWING THE FUTURE, AND CONTROLLING THE FUTURE

1. "Robert Fitzroy and the 'Evolution' of Weather Forecasting," *The Shelf: Preserving Harvard's Library Collections*, May 20, 2012, https://archive.blogs .harvard.edu/preserving/2012/05/20/robert-fitzroy-and-the-evolution-of -weather-forecasting/.

2. John Markoff, "Seeking a Better Way to Find Web Images," *New York Times*, November 19, 2012, https://www.nytimes.com/2012/11/20/science /for-web-images-creating-new-technology-to-seek-and-find.html.

3. "Meta Ad Revenue (2009–2023)," *Oberlo*, accessed November 22, 2024, https://www.oberlo.com/statistics/meta-advertising-revenue; "Google Ad Revenue (2013–2027)," *Oberlo*, accessed November 22, 2024, https://www .oberlo.com/statistics/google-ad-revenue.

4. Shoshana Zuboff, *The Age of Surveillance Capitalism* (New York: Public-Affairs, 2019).

5. Cecilia Rikap, *Capitalism, Power and Innovation: Intellectual Monopoly Capitalism Uncovered* (New York: Routledge, 2021).

9. ARTIFICIAL INTELLIGENCE AND THE CALCULUS OF HUMAN DEPENDENCE

1. "Artificial Intelligence Coined at Dartmouth," Dartmouth College, accessed October 6, 2024, https://home.dartmouth.edu/about/artificial -intelligence-ai-coined-dartmouth.

2. Nils J. Nilsson, *The Quest for Artificial Intelligence* (Cambridge: Cambridge University Press, 2009).

3. Nilsson, *The Quest for Artificial Intelligence*.

4. Nilsson, *The Quest for Artificial Intelligence*.

5. Warren S. McCulloch and Walter Pitts, "A Logical Calculus of the Ideas Immanent in Nervous Activity," *Bulletin of Mathematical Biophysics* 52, no. 1/2 (1943).

6. Frank Rosenblatt, "The Perceptron: A Probabilistic Model for Information Storage and Organization in the Brain," *Psychological Review* 65, no. 6 (1958).

7. "New Navy Device Learns by Doing," *New York Times*, July 8, 1958, https:// www.nytimes.com/1958/07/08/archives/new-navy-device-learns-by-doing -psychologist-shows-embryo-of.html.

8. Cade Metz, *Genius Makers: The Mavericks Who Brought AI to Google, Facebook, and the World* (New York: Dutton, 2021).

9. Most significantly, the inability to imitate an XOR gate, which returns a 1 when only one input is a 1, but not both. The ultimate solution was a multilayer Perceptron with a backpropagation algorithm, but that solution was described only in 1986.

10. "AlexNet and ImageNet: The Birth of Deep Learning," *Pinecone*, accessed November 22, 2024, https://www.pinecone.io/learn/series/image-search /imagenet/.

11. Gary Marcus, "Is 'Deep Learning' a Revolution in Artificial Intelligence?,"

New Yorker, November 25, 2012, https://www.newyorker.com/news/news
-desk/is-deep-learning-a-revolution-in-artificial-intelligence.

12. Cade Metz, "'The Godfather of A.I.' Leaves Google and Warns of Danger
    Ahead," *New York Times*, May 4, 2023, https://www.nytimes.com/2023/05
    /01/technology/ai-google-chatbot-engineer-quits-hinton.html.

13. Jeremy Li, "ChatGPT in a Nutshell," *Medium*, July 14, 2023, https://
    medium.com/@lijo61703/chatgpt-in-a-nutshell-37ea5ddbc362.

14. "AI Chatbots: Energy Usage of 2023's Most Popular Chatbots (So Far),"
    TRG Datacenters, accessed November 22, 2024, https://www.trgdatacenters
    .com/resource/ai-chatbots-energy-usage-of-2023s-most-popular-chatbots
    -so-far/.

15. "Statement on AI Risk," Center for AI Safety, May 30, 2024, https://www
    .safe.ai/work/statement-on-ai-risk.

16. Rakesh Kochhar, "Which U.S. Workers Are More Exposed to AI on Their
    Jobs?," Pew Research Center, July 26, 2023, https://www.pewresearch.org
    /social-trends/2023/07/26/which-u-s-workers-are-more-exposed-to-ai-on
    -their-jobs/.

17. Martin Obschonka et al., "In the Shadow of Coal: How Large-Scale Indus-
    tries Contributed to Present-Day Regional Differences in Personality and
    Well-Being," *Journal of Personality and Social Psychology* 115, no. 5 (2018).

18. Tim Wu, "In an AI Future, We Will All Be Middle Managers," *Globe and
    Mail*, April 21, 2023, https://www.theglobeandmail.com/opinion/article-in
    -an-ai-future-we-are-all-middle-managers/.

19. Douglas B. Grisaffe and Hieu P. Nguyen, "Antecedents of Emotional
    Attachment to Brand," *Journal of Business Research* 64, no. 10 (2011).

20. "GPT-4o System Card," OpenAI, August 8, 2024, https://openai.com
    /index/gpt-4o-system-card/.

21. Asburydin, Reddit, accessed November 22, 2024.

22. Nilay Patel, "Replika CEO Eugenia Kuyda Says It's Okay If We End Up
    Marrying AI Chatbots," *The Verge*, August 12, 2024.

10. PLATFORM POWER BEYOND TECH

1. "NHE Fact Sheet," Centers for Medicare and Medicaid Services, accessed
   October 7, 2024, https://www.cms.gov/data-research/statistics-trends-and
   -reports/national-health-expenditure-data/nhe-fact-sheet.

2. "Oil and Gas Industry Revenue in the United States from 2010 to 2023,"
   Statista, October 4, 2024, https://www.statista.com/statistics/294614
   /revenue-of-the-gas-and-oil-industry-in-the-us/.

3. "U.S. Motor Vehicle and Parts Advanced Retail Trade Revenue 2000–
   2023," Statista, July 15, 2024, https://www.statista.com/statistics/531522
   /revenue-of-us-motor-vehicle-and-parts-retail-trade/.

4. Jane M. Zhu, Lynn M. Hua, and Daniel Polsky, "Private Equity Acquisitions of Physical Medical Groups Across Specialties, 2013–2016," *Journal
   of the American Medical Association* 323, no. 7 (2020).

5. Richard M. Scheffler et al., "Monetizing Medicine: Private Equity and
   Competition in Physician Practice Markets," American Antitrust Insti-

tute, July 10, 2023, https://www.antitrustinstitute.org/wp-content/uploads
/2023/07/AAI-UCB-EG_Private-Equity-I-Physician-Practice-Report
_FINAL.pdf.

6. Amelia M. Bond et al., "An Uptick in Pricing by Anesthesiologists: What
Role Do Management Companies Play?," Columbia University Mailman
School of Public Health, February 28, 2022, https://www.publichealth
.columbia.edu/news/uptick-pricing-anesthesiologists-what-role-do
-management-companies-play.

7. Chad Terhune, "Life-Threatening Heart Attack Leaves Teacher with
$108,951 Bill," NPR, August 27, 2018, https://www.npr.org/sections
/health-shots/2018/08/27/640891882/life-threatening-heart-attack-leaves
-teacher-with-108-951-bill.

8. Peter Whoriskey, "Financiers Bought Up Anesthesia Practices, Then Raised
Prices," Washington Post, June 29, 2023, https://www.washingtonpost.com
/business/2023/06/29/private-equity-medical-practices-raise-prices/.

9. Whoriskey, "Financiers Bought Up Anesthesia Practices, Then Raised
Prices."

10. Scheffler et al., "Monetizing Medicine: Private Equity and Competition in
Physician Practice Markets."

11. Alexander Borsa et al., "Evaluating Trends in Private Equity Ownership and Impacts and Health Outcomes, Costs, and Quality: Systematic
Review," BMJ (Clinical research ed.) 382 (2023).

12. Daniel Indiviglio, "2010 Set a New Record for Foreclosure Activity," The
Atlantic, January 13, 2011, https://www.theatlantic.com/business/archive
/2011/01/2010-set-a-new-record-for-foreclosure-activity/69472/; Fran-
cesca Mari, "A $60 Billion Housing Grab by Wall Street," New York
Times Magazine, October 22, 2021, https://www.nytimes.com/2020/03/04
/magazine/wall-street-landlords.html.

13. Michael Hout and Erin Cumberworth, "The Labor Force and the Great
Recession," Stanford Center on Poverty and Inequality, October 2012,
https://inequality.stanford.edu/sites/default/files/LaborMarkets_fact_sheet
.pdf.

14. Donald Trump, How to Build a Fortune (New York: Vanguard Press, 2006).

15. Alex Crippen, "Warren Buffett on CNBC: I'd Buy Up 'A Couple Hundred
Thousand' Single-Family Homes If I Could," CNBC, February 27, 2012,
https://www.cnbc.com/2012/02/27/warren-buffett-on-cnbc-id-buy-up-a
-couple-hundred-thousand-singlefamily-homes-if-i-could.html.

16. Jonathan O'Connell, Peter Whoriskey, and Kevin Schaul, "At Invitation
Homes, Unpermitted Work Leaves Leaky Plumbing, Faulty Repairs, Renters Say," Washington Post, July 12, 2022, https://www.washingtonpost.com
/business/2022/07/12/invitation-homes-corporate-landlord-permits/.

17. Brad Greiwe, "The Institutionalization of an Emerging Asset Class: The
Origin Story of Invitation Homes," Medium, August 10, 2017, https://
medium.com/fifth-wall-insights/the-institutionalization-of-an-emerging
-asset-class-the-origin-story-of-invitation-homes-1f949603a231.

18. Greiwe, "The Institutionalization of an Emerging Asset Class: The Origin
Story of Invitation Homes."

19. Mari, "A $60 Billion Housing Grab by Wall Street."

20. Zaidee Stavely, "From Foreclosure to Eviction: One Family's Struggle to Recover," *KQED*, July 7, 2017, https://www.kqed.org/news/11465371/from-foreclosure-to-eviction-one-familys-struggle-to-recover.

21. Mari, "A $60 Billion Housing Grab by Wall Street."

22. Brett Christophers, "How and Why U.S. Single-Housing Became an Investor Asset Class," *Journal of Urban History* 49, no. 2 (2021).

23. Greiwe, "The Institutionalization of an Emerging Asset Class: The Origin Story of Invitation Homes."

24. Greiwe, "The Institutionalization of an Emerging Asset Class: The Origin Story of Invitation Homes."

25. "Report Claims Larger Landlords Exploiting Tenants, Harming Neighborhoods," *CBS Sacramento*, January 18, 2018, https://www.cbsnews.com/sacramento/news/report-larger-landlords-exploit-tenants/; Meredith Abood, "Securitizing Suburbia: The Financialization of Single-Family Rental Housing and the 'Need' to Redefine 'Risk,'" Thesis: M.C.P., Massachusetts Institute of Technology, Department of Urban Studies and Planning, 2017.

26. Gavin Off, "NC Corporate Landlord Tenants Must Decide: Take Cash or Challenge Company Solo?," *Charlotte Observer*, March 18, 2024, https://www.charlotteobserver.com/news/business/real-estate-news/article286730260.html.

27. "Lease Easy Bundle," Invitation Homes, accessed October 9, 2024, https://www.invitationhomes.com/lease-easy.

28. "FTC Takes Action Against Invitation Homes for Deceiving Renters, Charging Junk Fees, Withholding Security Deposits, and Employing Unfair Eviction Practices," Federal Trade Commission, September 24, 2024, https://www.ftc.gov/news-events/news/press-releases/2024/09/ftc-takes-action-against-invitation-homes-deceiving-renters-charging-junk-fees-withholding-security.

29. "Pet-Friendly Homes," Invitation Homes, accessed October 9, 2024, https://www.invitationhomes.com/pet-friendly-homes-for-lease.

30. Jennifer Kraus, "Former Tenants Share Horror Stories of Renting from Real Estate Investment Firm Invitation Homes," *News Channel 5 | Nashville*, February 4, 2019, https://www.newschannel5.com/news/newschannel-5-investigates/former-tenants-share-horror-stories-of-renting-from-real-estate-investment-firm-invitation-homes.

31. Mari, "A $60 Billion Housing Grab by Wall Street."

32. Abood, "Securitizing Suburbia: The Financialization of Single-Family Rental Housing and the 'Need' to Redefine 'Risk.'"

33. Rebekah L. Sanders and Catherine Reagor, "'Stay Away': Arizona Families Share Horror Stories of One of Arizona's Largest Landlords," *Arizona Republic*, August 15, 2018.

34. O'Connell, Whoriskey, and Schaul, "At Invitation Homes, Unpermitted Work Leaves Leaky Plumbing, Faulty Repairs, Renters Say."

35. "Market Capitalization of Invitation Homes (INVH)," Companies Market Cap, accessed November 22, 2024, https://companiesmarketcap.com/invitation-homes/marketcap/#:~:text=Market%20cap%3A%20%2418.94%20Billion%20USD,cap%20according%20to%20our%20data.

36. Additional_Treat_181, "Increase Your Budget. They Have a Stated Business Plan: Buy up Houses in Lower Income Communities, Jack up Rents, Have a Monopoly," Reddit, accessed November 22, 2024.

37. "US FTC Fines Invitation Homes $48 Million over Hidden Fees," Reuters, September 24, 2024, https://www.reuters.com/markets/us/us-ftc-reaches-48-million-settlement-with-invitation-homes-over-junk-fees-costs-2024-09-24/#:~:text=Sept%2024%20(Reuters)%20%2D%20Invitation,deceived%20renters%20about%20lease%20costs.

38. John Adams to James Sullivan, May 26, 1776, National Archives Founders Online, https://founders.archives.gov/documents/Adams/06-04-02-0091.

39. "Invitation Homes (INVH)—Total Assets," Companies Market Cap, accessed November 22, 2024, https://companiesmarketcap.com/invitation-homes/total-assets/.

40. "Number of Renter Occupied Housing Units in the United States from 1975 to 2023," Statista, September 4, 2023, https://www.statista.com/statistics/187577/housing-units-occupied-by-renter-in-the-us-since-1975/#:~:text=Number%20of%20renter%20occupied%20homes%20in%20the%20U.S.%201975%2D2023&text=In%202023%2C%20there%20were%20approximately,term%20upward%20swing%20since%201975.; "U.S. Housing Market Nears $50 Trillion in Value as Number of Trillion-Dollar Metros Doubles," Redfin Investor Relations, August 8, 2024, https://investors.redfin.com/news-events/press-releases/detail/1149/u-s-housing-market-nears-50-trillion-in-value-as-number#:~:text=%E2%80%9CThe%20value%20of%20America's%20housing,Economics%20Research%20Lead%20Chen%20Zhao.

PART III: THE DANGERS OF CENTRALIZED ECONOMIC POWER

1. Thomas Carothers and Benjamin Press, "Understanding and Responding to Global Democratic Backsliding," Carnegie Endowment for International Peace, October 20, 2022, https://carnegieendowment.org/research/2022/10/understanding-and-responding-to-global-democratic-backsliding?lang=en.

2. Francis Fukuyama, *The End of History and the Last Man* (New York: Free Press, 1992).

11. ECONOMIC MANIA

1. Jon Henley, "Haiti: A Long Descent to Hell," *The Guardian*, January 14, 2010, https://www.theguardian.com/world/2010/jan/14/haiti-history-earthquake-disaster.

2. Richard Pares, *Merchants and Planters* (Cambridge: Cambridge University, 1960).

3. Henley, "Haiti: A Long Descent to Hell."

4. "Remember Haiti: Economy," John Carter Brown Library, accessed October 16, 2024, https://www.brown.edu/Facilities/John_Carter_Brown_Library/exhibitions/remember_haiti/race.php.

5. Stewart R. King, *Blue Coat or Powdered Wig: Free People of Color in Pre-Revolutionary Saint Domingue* (Athens: University of Georgia Press, 2001).
6. King, *Blue Coat or Powdered Wig: Free People of Color in Pre-Revolutionary Saint Domingue*.
7. Angela Naimou, "'I NEED MANY REPETITIONS': Rehearsing the Haitian Revolution in the Shadows of the Sugar Mill," *Callaloo* 35, no. 1 (2012).
8. Alexander D. Barder, *Global Race War: International Politics and Racial Hierarchy* (Oxford: Oxford University Press, 2021).
9. Diana Roy and Rocio Cara Labrador, "Haiti's Troubled Path to Development," Council on Foreign Relations, June 25, 2024, https://www.cfr.org/backgrounder/haitis-troubled-path-development.
10. Robert A. Schneider, *The Return of Resentment: The Rise and Decline and Rise Again of a Political Emotion* (Chicago: Chicago University Press, 2023).

12. SOME SOLUTIONS

1. Lawrence J. Baack, "Agrarian Reform in Eighteenth-Century Denmark," *University Studies of the University of Nebraska*, no. 56 (1977).
2. Baack, "Agrarian Reform in Eighteenth-Century Denmark."
3. Baack, "Agrarian Reform in Eighteenth-Century Denmark."
4. Baack, "Agrarian Reform in Eighteenth-Century Denmark."
5. Nina Siegal, "A Heritage Amsterdam Show Looks Closer at Catherine the Great," *New York Times*, September 8, 2016, https://www.nytimes.com/2016/09/08/arts/international/a-hermitage-amsterdam-show-looks-closer-at-catherine-the-great.html#:~:text=As%20Catherine%20wrote%20in%20her,subjects%20happiness%2C%20liberty%20and%20prosperity.
6. Robert K. Massie, *Portrait of a Woman: The Life of Catherine the Great* (New York: Random House, 2011).
7. Massie, *Portrait of a Woman: The Life of Catherine the Great*.
8. Ekaterina Zhuravskaya and Andrei Markevich, "Economic Effects of the Abolition of Serfdom: Evidence from the Russian Empire," Centre for Economic Policy Research (2015).
9. Terrence Prittie, "The Krupp Empire," *The Atlantic*, October 1960, https://www.theatlantic.com/magazine/archive/1960/10/the-krupp-empire/658504/.
10. Ian Kershaw, *Hitler: 1889–1936 Hubris* (New York: W. W. Norton, 1998).
11. U.S. Congress, Senate, Committee on Military Affairs, Subcommittee on War Mobilization, *Cartels and National Security: Report Pursuant to S. Res. 107*, 78th Cong., 2d sess., 1944, Subcomm. Rep., 4, 8.
12. U.S. Congress, Senate, *Hearings Before the Subcommittee of the Committee on Appropriations*, 80th Cong., 1st sess., July 19, 1948.
13. Mancur Olson, *The Rise and Decline of Nations: Economic Growth, Stagflation, and Social Rigidities* (New Haven, CT: Yale University Press, 1982).
14. Hsiao-Ting Lin, *Accidental State: Chiang Kai-shek, the United States, and the Making of Taiwan* (Cambridge, MA: Harvard University Press, 2016).

15. Samuel D. Warren and Louis D. Brandeis, "The Right to Privacy," *Harvard Law Review* 4, no. 5 (1890).

13. THE PERSISTENT DREAM OF THE SELF-CORRECTING ECONOMY

1. Thomas K. McCraw, "Joseph Schumpeter on Competition," *Competition Policy International* 8, no. 1 (2012).
2. John Kenneth Galbraith, "The Essential Galbraith," Library of Congress, accessed October 11, 2024, https://catdir.loc.gov/catdir/samples/hm051/2001024986.html.
3. "Union Members—2023," Bureau of Labor Statistics, January 23, 2024, https://www.bls.gov/news.release/pdf/union2.pdf.
4. Thomas Piketty, *Capital in the Twenty-First Century* (Cambridge, MA: Harvard University Press, 2014).

14. ARTIFICIAL INTELLIGENCE AND CRYPTO: THE TECHNOLOGICAL ANSWERS TO ECONOMIC INEQUALITY

1. "Advancing Decentralization," worldcoin.org, December 6, 2023, https://worldcoin.org/blog/foundational-topics/advancing-decentralization.
2. Anthony Clarke, "How Cryptocurrency Could Help Tackle Global Income Inequality," *Cointelegraph*, August 31, 2022, https://cointelegraph.com/news/how-cryptocurrency-could-help-tackle-global-income-inequality.
3. "For Every Human," *Worldcoins*, accessed October 9, 2024, https://www.worldcions.com/#/.
4. Vinamrata Chaturvedi, "Everything to Know About Bitcoin Pizza Day," *Quartz*, May 19, 2024, https://qz.com/bitcoin-pizza-day-date-origin-history-cryptocurrency-1851481975#:~:text=On%20May%2022%2C%202010%2C%20a,revolution%20brought%20about%20by%20cryptocurrency.
5. Guneet Kaur, "The Mt. Gox Bitcoin Heist, and Why It Still Matters," *Cointelegraph*, June 26, 2024, https://cointelegraph.com/learn/the-mt-gox-bitcoin-heist.
6. Robert McMillan, "The Inside Story of Mt. Gox, Bitcoin's $460 Million Disaster," *Wired*, March 3, 2014, https://www.wired.com/2014/03/bitcoin-exchange/.
7. Faruk Fatih Ozer, "Thodex Cryptocurrency Boss Jailed for 11,196 Years in Turkey for Fraud," *BBC*, September 8, 2023, https://www.bbc.com/news/world-europe-66752785.
8. Tom Blackstone, "Bitcoin ETFs Are 'Stepping Away from the Ideals' of Crypto," *Cointelegraph*, January 19, 2024, https://cointelegraph.com/news/bitcoin-etfs-stepping-away-ideals-crypto-blockchain-execs.
9. Oscar Lopez and Ephrat Livni, "In Global First, El Salvador Adopts Bitcoin as Currency," *New York Times*, September 7, 2021, https://www.nytimes.com/2021/09/07/world/americas/el-salvador-bitcoin.html.
10. Robert Hart, "What Is Worldcoin?," *Forbes*, July 24, 2023, https://www

.forbes.com/sites/roberthart/2023/07/24/what-is-worldcoin-heres-what
-to-know-about-the-eyeball-scanning-crypto-project-launched-by
-openais-sam-altman/.

15. MERE REDISTRIBUTION

1. Paul R. La Monica, "Apple Has $203 Billion in Cash. Why?," *CNN*, July 22, 2015, https://money.cnn.com/2015/07/22/investing/apple-stock -cash-earnings/.

16. PLATFORMS AND THE ARCHITECTURE OF EQUALITY

1. Ben Thompson, "Is the Internet Different?," *Stratechery*, November 3, 2020, https://stratechery.com/2020/is-the-internet-different/?utm_source =Memberful&utm_campaign=95d9f5bfdb-daily_update_2020_11_03& utm_medium=email&utm_term=0_d4c7fece27-95d9f5bfdb-111330179.
2. John Cannon, *The Oxford Companion to British History* (Oxford: Oxford University Press, 2009).
3. "Unions Help Reduce Disparities and Strengthen Our Democracy," Economic Policy Institute, April 23, 2021, https://www.epi.org/publication /unions-help-reduce-disparities-and-strengthen-our-democracy/.
4. "Unions Help Reduce Disparities and Strengthen Our Democracy."
5. Juhohn Lee, "Why American Wages Haven't Grown Despite Increases in Productivity," *CNBC*, July 19, 2022, https://www.cnbc.com/2022/07/19 /heres-how-labor-dynamism-affects-wage-growth-in-america.html.
6. Michael W. L. Elsby, Bart Hobijn, and Aysegul Sahin, "The Decline of the U.S. Labor Share," Brookings Institution, July 2016, https://www .brookings.edu/wp-content/uploads/2016/07/2013b_elsby_labor_share .pdf.
7. Quoctrung Bui, "50 Years of Shrinking Union Membership, in One Map," NPR, February 23, 2015, https://www.npr.org/sections/money/2015/02 /23/385843576/50-years-of-shrinking-union-membership-in-one-map.
8. Elana Prager and Matt Schmitt, "Employer Consolidation and Wages: Evidence from Hospitals," *American Economic Review* 111, no. 2 (2021).
9. Denny Strigl, "Labor Unions Are Obsolete," *Managers, can you hear me now?*, February 11, 2012, https://managerscanyouhearmenow.wordpress .com/2012/02/11/labor-unions-are-obsolete/.
10. Tim Sackett, "Labor Unions Are Dinosaurs," *The Tim Sackett Project*, February 27, 2015, https://timsackett.com/2015/02/#:~:text=I%20just%20don 't%20see,afford%20to%20treat%20employees%20bad.
11. "Hearings Before the Committee on Investigation of United States Steel Corporation," Government Printing Office, January 12, 1912, https://www .google.com/books/edition/UNITED_STATES_STEEL _CORPORATION/NDEsAAAAMAAJ?hl=en&gbpv=0.
12. Theron Mohamed, "Warren Buffett's Toll Roads, Elon Musk's Bottlenecks,

and Why Both Men Prize the Same Kinds of Businesses," *Business Insider*, September 2, 2023, https://markets.businessinsider.com/news/stocks /warren-buffett-elon-musk-toll-roads-bottlenecks-tesla-spacex-starlink -2023-9.

13. "Connections North: Bridges of the West End," West End Museum, accessed October 11, 2024, https://thewestendmuseum.org/exhibits /connections-north-bridges-of-the-west-end/.

14. Evelyn Atkinson, *The "People's Bridge": Popular Sovereignty and the Charles River Bridge Case*, Stigler Center New Working Paper Series no. 25, June 2018, https://www.econstor.eu/bitstream/10419/262682/1/wp280.pdf.

15. "Residential Energy Consumption Survey (RECS)," US Energy Information Administration, accessed October 11, 2024, https://www.eia.gov /consumption/residential/data/2020/index.php?view=consumption&src=< %20Consumption%20%20%20%20%20%20Residential%20Energy %20Consumption%20Survey%20(RECS)-f3#summary.

16. Matt Rej, "The Complete Guide to Amex Interchange Rates and Processing Fees," Merchant Cost Consulting, May 2, 2024, https://merchant costconsulting.com/lower-credit-card-processing-fees/the-complete -guide-to-amex-interchange-and-processing-fees/#:~:text=As%20of %20July%201%2C%202022,—%203.01%25%20+%20$0.10%20per %20transaction.

17. Jack Caporal, "Average Credit Card Processing Fees and Costs in 2024," *The Motley Fool*, Aug. 28, 2024, https://www.fool.com/the-ascent/research /average-credit-card-processing-fees-costs-america/.

18. "EU Regulator Accepts Visa Europe's Credit Fee Cap Offer," Reuters, February 26, 2014, https://www.reuters.com/article/world/americas/eu-regulator -accepts-visa-europe-s-credit-fee-cap-offer-idUSL6N0LV23W/.

INDEX

A NOTE ABOUT THE AUTHOR

Tim Wu is the Julius Silver Professor of Law, Science and Technology at Columbia Law School. He served as special assistant to the president for technology and competition policy under the Biden administration, worked on competition policy in the Obama White House and the Federal Trade Commission, and served as senior enforcement counsel at the New York attorney general's office. The author of *The Master Switch* and *The Attention Merchants*, he lives in New York City.

A NOTE ON THE TYPE

This book was set in Janson, a typeface long thought to have been made by the Dutchman Anton Janson, who was a practicing typefounder in Leipzig during the years 1668–1687. However, it has been conclusively demonstrated that these types are actually the work of Nicholas Kis (1650–1702), a Hungarian, who most probably learned his trade from the master Dutch typefounder Dirk Voskens. The type is an excellent example of the influential and sturdy Dutch types that prevailed in England up to the time William Caslon (1692–1766) developed his own incomparable designs from them.

Typeset by Scribe,
Philadelphia, Pennsylvania

Designed by Soonyoung Kwon